A World New to Some

Dr. Gordon McCrea Fisher, Ph.D.

Contents

1. Puritan Preacher 1
2. Witchcraft 4
3. Samuel, Jr.'s Letter 7
4. Early Wethersfield, CT 9
5. Indians 11
6. Rev. Henry's Troubles 12
7. The Pequot War 15
8. Evaluations 18
9. Samuel Hale after the Pequot War 29
10. Samuel Hale, Jr., Justice of the Peace 32
11. Wethersfield and her Daughters 33
12. Gov. Thomas Welles and the Fundamental Orders 37
13. Jonathan Hale I, II, and III 48
14. Endnotes 52

A World New to Some

Gordon Fisher

gmfisher7@optonline.net

For, after all, gentle reader, cities of themselves, and, in fact, empires of themselves, are nothing without an historian.
Washington Irving, *Knickerbocker's History of New York*, 1809

History, n. An account mostly false, of events mostly unimportant, which are brought about by rulers mostly knaves, and soldiers mostly fools.
Ambrose Bierce, *The Devil's Dictionary,* 1906.

Rev. Henry Smith

1. Puritan Preacher.

The Reverend Henry Smith arrived in New England in 1635 or 1636 (or 1637), when he was about 48 years old. He was, according to the genealogist Henry Stiles, the first settled pastor at Wethersfield CT. Stiles says:

In 1641, after [Peter] Prudden, [Roger] Sherman and [Richard] Denton had, one after another, ministered to the people, and had each passed away to more quiet fields of labor, Wethersfield, for the first time, became possessed of a *settled* minister in the person of the Rev. Henry Smith, who is described as 'a gentleman of good family,' and one who, 'as the patriarch of one of the best sustained and accomplished families in New England, is entitled to our regard as a gentleman of uncommon culture, refinement and firmness.' With his wife and several small children, he is supposed to have arrived [in Wethersfield]in 1639, if not earlier — probably from Charlestown, Mass., where he had arrived in 1637, from England.

The genealogist James Savage says that maybe Rev. Henry arrived in 1635 on the Elizabeth, or maybe he didn't. The Rev. Alonzo Chapin stated in his centennial discourse of 1853 on Glastenbury CT (nowadays, Glastonbury with an "o") that Rev. Henry probably arrived in 1637, since it was in December of that year that he and his wife Dorothy joined the church in Charlestown MA , or perhaps in Watertown MA. The genealogists Donald Lines Jacobus and Edgar Francis Waterman say that the Rev. Henry did not arrive in 1635 on the Elizabeth, and that it must have been a different Henry

Smith who joined the church at Watertown with his wife Dorothy. So it goes in genealogical research.

There was at least one other Henry Smith who came from Old to New England in the Great Migration with John Winthrop's fleet in 1630. Very likely this other Henry Smith was the one who married the daughter Anne (or Ann) of the noted merchant William Pynchon, who also came over with Winthrop's fleet. Winthrop was the administrative leader of the immigrants, not the captain of the fleet. He became the first governor of the Massachusetts Bay Colony, and it was he who characterized the colony-to-be as a "Citty upon a Hill, the eyes of all people are uppon us". [1]

Samuel Smith, a son of Rev. Henry, said in a letter of 1 January 1699 (old style) that his father arrived in Watertown MA from England in 1636 (or 1637, although others say he arrived in Charlestown first, and then removed to Watertown. [2]

Rev. Henry died in 1648, when Samuel was about 10 years old. Samuel's letter describing his father was written when Samuel was 61, and he starts this letter to his son Ichabod by remarking that he was at so tender an age when Rev. Henry died, that he had only a little of the information Ichabod had requested.

In any case, it seems as certain as such matters can be that a Henry Smith did become the first settled minister at Wethersfield CT in 1637. The historian Mary Jeanne Anderson Jones says:

The ecclesiastical leaders of the exodus [to New England] **were Puritan ministers like Thomas Hooker, Samuel Stone, John Warham, Ephraim Huit, and Henry Smith, who had been preachers of note in England. The majority of them were alumni of Emmanuel College, Cambridge, where Puritanism was rampant.**

Henry's son Samuel, in the letter alluded to before, says his father was a graduate of Cambridge. Jacobus and Waterman (the genealogists) say that he **"may have been the Henry Smith who matriculated from Kings College, Cambridge, A.B., 1619/20; Fellow of Kings."** The genealogist Frederick Lewis Weis in his work on the colonial clergy of New England is more definite:

Henry Smith, A.M., b. Norwich, England, 1588; matric. Sidney Sussex Coll., Camb., 1617; Magdalene Coll., Camb., A.B., 1621/2; A.M., 1625; Ord. by the Bishop of Peterborough, June 8, 1623; sett. Watertown, 1636/7; sett. Wethersfield, Ct., 1641-1648, as the first minister; d. Wethersfield, Ct., 1648.

The genealogist Henry Stiles has a footnote (1904) on the possible origin of our Rev. Henry (which contradicts Jacobus and Waterman). Stiles says one account of Rev. Henry holds him to have been from Blaby, co. Leicester, England, and that he was son of Erastus or Erasmus (the indecision is Stiles's) Smith who married (1) a Miss Bydd (could it have been Byrd?), and (2) about 1576, Margaret Cecil, daughter of William Cecil, Lord Burleigh, Elizabeth I's prime minister, and widow of Roger Case (or Cave)(or Carr). Presumably Henry's mother was Miss Bydd, and not Margaret Cecil.

2. Witchcraft.

At the time of Rev. Henry's tenure in the pulpit at Wethersfield CT, witchcraft was a popular endeavor, or perhaps I should say accusations of witchcraft were popular. Witchcraft as practiced in Connecticut and Massachusetts appears to have migrated to New England along with the original invaders from the Old Country. It was occasionally lethal to its practitioners and sometimes, it was said, to those on which it was practiced.

The trial of Alse Young

The historian William DeLoss Love wrote:The most serious indictment that has ever been brought against our early criminal courts is for their action in the witchcraft delusion, the explanation of which has been often made and is here left to others. It was an episode in New England history that should be judged in view of similar beliefs then current in the old world. In Connecticut, all the cases where the condemned were executed occurred between 1647 and 1662. They were, therefore, tried in the Particular Court. Of the seventeen in the river towns who were charged with witchcraft during this period, nine were residents of Hartford. Three of these were executed. As the prison where all criminals of Hartford, Windsor, Wethersfield and Farmington were confined was located in Hartford, it is probable that the entire number from these towns, which were hung in this delusion, suffered in Hartford. Alse Young of Windsor was the first unhappy victim, but the court records give us no information concerning her trial. On the cover of Mathew Grant's Diary, Dr. J. Hammond Trumbull discovered the record "May 26, [16]47 Alse Young was hanged." This supplies the blank in Winthrop's History: "One —— —— of Windsor arraigned and executed at Hartford for a witch." So far as known, this was the first execution for witchcraft in New England. The next victim was Mary Johnson of Wethersfield . In 1646, she had been sentenced to be whipped for theft, probably at Hartford, which was to be repeated a month later at Wethersfield. On her own confession, she was indicted by a jury December 7, 1648, as guilty of "familiarity with the Deuill." Mather says, "Her confession was attended with such convictive circumstances that it could not be slighted." She confessed, he says, that she had murdered a child, and committed other faults of licentiousness. For some months before her execution, she was imprisoned at Hartford, under the care of William Ruscoe. A son was born to her while there. Nathaniel Ruscoe, the jailor's son, agreed with her before her death to bring up and educate the child, which agreement was afterward sanctioned by the court. The jailor was paid L6 10s, for twenty-four weeks' charges to June 6, 1650, from which fact it is inferred that she was executed on that date. Rev. Samuel Stone ministered to her while in prison, and it is said that she became a penitent woman. She was evidently a poor, misguided creature, who accounted for her fault according to the superstition of the age.

Rev. Samuel Stone

How many months was she in prison? Was the jailer's son the father of the child? She is, so says the historian John Putnam Demos, on the whole "**a historical phantom, impossible to study, or portray, in three-dimensional detail.**"

Cotton Mather said in 1689 (some 40 years after the event) that Mary Johnson testified

..... that a devil was wont to do her many services. Her master blamed her for not carrying out the ashes, and a devil did clear the hearth for her afterwards. Her master sending her into the field, to drive out the hogs that used to break into it, a devil would scour them out, and make her laugh to see how he feazed [drove] 'em about." "Her first familiarity with the devils," says Mather, **"came by discontent; and wishing the devil to take that and t'other thing; and, the devil to do this and that; whereupon a devil appeared unto her, tendering her the best service he could do for her.**

Cotton Mather

It appears that not only does the devil find work for idle hands, he (or subordinate devils) also works for servants on demand.

According to Mather:

In the time of her imprisonment, the famous Mr. Samuel Stone was at great pains to promote her conversion unto God, and represent unto her both her misery and remedy," apparently with some success, since **"she died in a frame extremely to the satisfaction of them that were spectators of it."**

In a proof of the existence of witchcraft, in his work of 1689 called *Memorable Providences, Relating to Witchcraft and Possessions*, Mather puts great weight on the confessions of witchcraft made by Mary Johnson and some others. He says: **"If such *Confessions* must be Ridiculed: all the *Murders*, yea all the *Bargains* in the World must be meer *Imaginations* if such *Confessions* are of no Account."** But he was, in a way, consoled by the existence of witches. From the existence of witches he deduced the existence of devils, since **"Those are the Objects that *Witches* converse withal."** And, he says, **"Since there are *Witches* and *Devils*, we may conclude that there are also *Immortal Souls*,"** since **"*Devils* would never contract with *Witches* for their Souls if there were no such things to become a prey unto them."**

In the manner of Puritan ministers in New England in those days, the Rev. Henry Smith presided in 1648 at the trial of Mary Johnson. [3] In the letter from Samuel, son of Henry, to Ichabod, son of Samuel, we learn that the Reverend Henry Smith of Wethersfield CT..... **came to this Land by reason of the Great Persecution by which the infamous Archbishop Laud and the Black Tom Tyrant (as Mr. Russell was always wont to call the Earl of Strafforde) did cause the reign of his Majestie Charles the Firste to loose favour in the sight of the people of England.**

Archbishop William Laud

Mr. Russell was the 2nd husband of Dorothy, Rev. Henry's 2nd wife. The faithful Earl of Strafford, advisor to the King, recruited an army in 1640 in Ireland ostensibly to oppose the Scots, who were rebelling at the time. He was accused of really intending to use it against the English Puritans. The charge was never proven, but he nevertheless lost his head in 1641, during the Puritan ascendancy in Britain. Archbishop William Laud was Charles's assiduous administrator of anti-Puritanism, and has been considered by some to have precipitated the English Civil War in 1640 by trying in 1637 to impose the liturgy of the Anglican prayer book on Scottish Presbyterians. It is sometimes said, by way of excuse, that he was only acting as the king's enforcer. Laud was impeached by the Puritans in 1640, imprisoned in 1641, and in 1645 he too had his head detached. These were some of the early accomplishments of the Long Parliament, which was intermittently in session for the 20 years from 1640-1660, the period of the Glorious Revolution, the English Civil War. The Long Parliament was summoned by Charles I to help him raise money to fight the Scots, but it didn't work out the way he intended.

3. Samuel, Jr.'s letter.

Samuel, Jr.'s letter continues:

Concerning of ye earlie days I can remember but little save Hardship. My Parents had broughte both Men Servants & Maid Servants from England, but ye Maids tarried not but till they got Married, ye wch was shortly, for there was great scarcity of Women in ye Colonies. Ye men did abide better. Onne of em had married onne of my Mother's Maids & they did come with us to Weathersfield, to our grate Comforte for some years, untill they had manny littel onnes of theire Owne. I do well remember ye Face & Figure of my Honoured Father. He was 5 foote, 10 inches talle & spare of builde, tho not leane. He was an Active as ye Red Skin Men & sinewy. His delight was in sportes of strengthe, & withe his owne Hands he did helpe to reare bothe our owne House & ye Firste Meetinge House of Weatherfield, wherein he preacht yeares too fewe. He was well Featured & Fresh favoured with faire Skin & longe curling Hair (as neare all of us have had) with a merrie eye & swete smilinge Mouthe, tho he coulde frowne sternlie eno' when need was. Ye firste Meeting House was solid mayde to withstande ye wicked onsaults of ye Red Skins. Its Foundations was laide in ye feare of ye Lord, but its Walls was truly laide in ye feare of ye Indians for many & grate was ye Terrors of em. I do minde me yt alle ye able-bodyed Men did work thereat & ye old and feeble did watch in turns to espie if any Salvages was in hidinge neare & every Man keept his Musket nighe to his hande. I do not myself remember any of ye Attacks mayde by large bodeys of Indians whilst we did remayne in Weathersfield, but did oftimes hear of em. Several Families wch did live back a ways from ye River was either Murderdt or Captivated in my Boyhood & we all did live in constant feare of ye like. My father ever declardt there would not be so much to feare iff ye Red-Skins was treated with such mixture of Justice & Authority as they cld understand, but iff he was living now he must see that wee can do naught but <u>fight</u> em & that right heavily.

After ye Red Skins ye grate Terror of our lives at Weathersfield & for many yeares after we had moved to Hadley to live was ye Wolves. Catamounts were bad eno' & so was ye Beares, but it was ye Wolves yt was ye worst. The noyse of theyre howlings was eno' to curdle ye bloode of ye stoutest & I have never seen ye man yt did not shiver at ye sounde of a Packe of em. What with ye way we hated em & ye goode money yt was offered for theyre Heads we do not heare em now so much, but when I do I feel again ye younge Hatred rising in my Blood & it is not a Sin because God mayde em to be hated. My Mother & Sister did each of em Kill more yan one of ye gray Howlers & once my oldest Sister shot a Beare yt came too neare ye House. He was a good Fatte onne & keept us all in meate for a good while. I guess one of her Daughters has got ye skinne. As most of ye Weathersfield settlers did come afoot throu ye Wilderness & brought with em such Things only as they did nost neede at ye firste, ye other Things was sent round from Boston in Vessels to come up the River to us. Some of the shippes did come safe to Weathersfield, but many were lost in a grate storm. Amongst em was onne wch held alle our Beste Things. A good many Yeares later, long after my Father had died of the grate Fever & my Mother had married Mr. Russell & moved to Hadley it was found yt some of our Things had been saved & keept in ye Forst wch is by ye River's Mouthe [Saybrook], & they was brought to us. Most of em was spoilt with Sea water and Moulde especially ye Bookes [Footnote by Juliana: 'My Father [Mr. Russell] hath one of these books — The Vision of Piers Plowman. It is so ruinated with damp and mould yt no one can read ye whole of it'] & ye Plate. If this there was no grate store, only ye Tankard, wch I have, and some Spoones, divided amongst my Sisters, wch was alle so black it was long before any could come to its owne colour agen, [& Mr. Russell did opine yt had not been so it might not have founde us agen, but he was sometimes a little shorte of ye Charity wch thinketh no Evil, at ye least I was wont to think so when his Hand was too heavy on my Shoulders & I remembered ye sweetnesse & ye Charity of my firste Father. ...]

4. Early Wethersfield, CT.

Such was life in the early days of Wethersfield CT, which is said to have been the first settlement by Europeans on the Connecticut River. In fact, Sherman Adams reports in the genealogical book by him and Henry Stiles that **"The Rev. Stephen Mix, settled minister of Wethersfield from 1694 to 1738, and born in New Haven in 1672, was of the opinion that Wethersfield was the 'oldest town on the river.'"** [4]

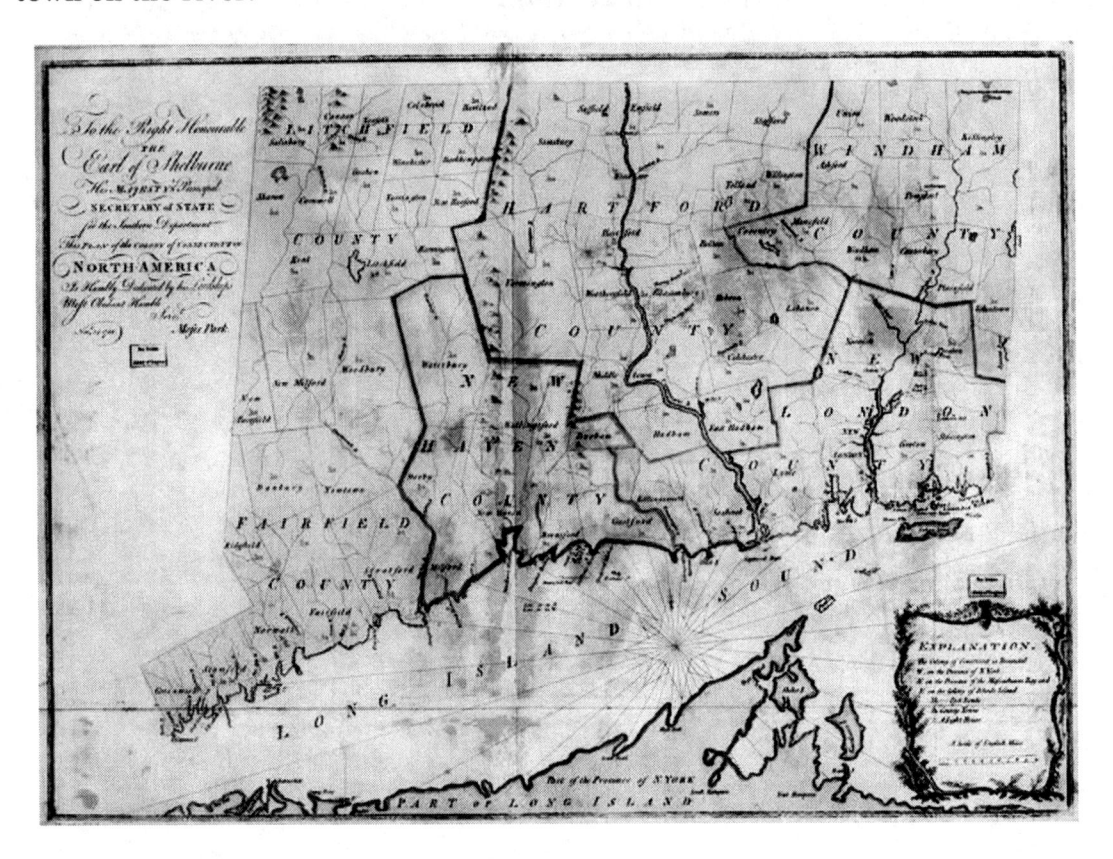

The first serious settlers (or *planters* as they said in those days) of Wethersfield migrated to the region in 1634 from Watertown MA, led by John Oldham. John Winthrop wrote in 1635 that "the occasion of their desire to remove, was, for that all towns in the Bay began to be much straitened by their own nearness to one another, and their cattle so much increased." In his edition of Winthrop's *Journal*, James Savage said "In this fifth year of the colony history [in Massachusetts] so sadly crowded was the settlement at Newton, that Watertown was not a mile and a half distant, nor Charlestown more than two miles." Already a population problem!

On the other hand, the New England historian William Hubbard "**who having been born in 1621, could well remember the Connecticut migration**" maintained that an "impulsive cause" which "**did secretly and powerfully drive on the business**" was a conflict of leading ministers, and that "**Two such eminent stars as were Mr. [Rev. John] Cotton and Mr. [Rev. Thomas] Hooker, both of the first magnitude, though of differing influence, could not well continue in one and the same orb.**"

Hooker and settlers leave for Connecticut

Viewed from the bottom up, so to speak, it was a population problem, and viewed from the top down a rivalry between two strong leaders. Perhaps the matter is better viewed as an interaction, with neither cause taking precedence over the other. That is, the people feeling crowded were willing to follow Hooker to Connecticut, and Hooker was happy to take advantage of this to separate himself from Cotton by leading some of the planters to Connecticut..

Adams was careful to give a legal definition of "town" made in 1628 by Sir Edmund Coke: "**It cannot be a town in law, unless it hath, or in past time hath had, a church and celebration of divine services, sacraments and burials.**" This pretty well leaves out Indians and earlier European explorers who may have camped awhile on the River. Actually, Adams remarks: "**That Indians either dwelt at, or frequented Pyquag, is very evident from their implements of war, the chase, domestic use, etc., which have been found on the plot which the settlers selected for their burying ground.**" *Pyquag* (or *Pyquaugh; Paquiaug, Puckquiog, Pua-qui-auke*, etc., meaning, according to Adams, "cleared land" or "open country") was an Indian name for the region which was renamed by the English first Watertown, and then soon after, Wethersfield.

5. Indians

Of the Indians, Adams observes that:

Rev. John Eliot preaching to the Indians

It is to be remembered that, in all these land purchases [by Englishmen from various Indians], **our forefathers seem to have acted in perfect honesty and good faith with the Indians. More than that, it is evident that they subsequently looked upon the former owners of the soil as, in a sense, their wards and needing their protection."** So, as you see, the Indians had nothing to worry about as their lands were taken away after what they appear to have understood to be gifts signaling friendship rather than payments for real estate. Besides, a great percentage of the Indians in this region died in these times of diseases imported from Europe, to which the Europeans were on the whole immune, which resulted in much land being vacated by them. Numerous Puritans took this as a sign that God was on their side. For example, in 1634, commenting on the smallpox epidemic in New England in 1633, John Winthrop wrote in a letter that by this epidemic **"God hath hereby cleared our title to this place,"** and in another letter that as **"for the natives, they are near all dead of the smallpox, so as the Lord hath cleared our title to what we possess.**

6. Rev. Henry's troubles.

The Rev. Henry Smith had more difficulties than those connected with house-building, Indians and bears, mentioned in his son's letter. There were unhappy souls in his church and congregation, and from the start he was a victim of unfounded suspicions and bitter accusations. Chief among his harassers was Clement Chaplin, who seems to have come to Wethersfield in 1636, before Rev. Henry, and was the "ruling elder" of the church when Rev. Henry took over. He held the office of Colonial Treasurer for the town. He appears to have been a cantankerous person. For example, he quarreled with the Town Recorder, Matthew Mitchell, in 1640, and by way of the General Court compelled Matthew to apologize to him publicly (over what, I don't know).

In 1643, the General Court appointed a committee to look into the discontent at the church in Wethersfield. In April the committee suggested that Rev. Henry resign as pastor "if yt may be done according to God." Rev. Henry apparently declined the invitation. In July, the Court requested that the charges be put in writing. In November, the Court announced that most of the charges against Rev. Henry were mistakes. They furthermore fined Clement Chaplin 10 pounds "for divulging and setting his hand to a paper called a declaration, tending to the defamation of Mr. Smith." Also fined various amounts were Francis Norton and John Goodridge for signing Chaplin's declaration, Mr. Plum for "preferring a roll of grievances against Mr. Smith, and failing of proof in the prosecution thereof," and Robert Rose for joining with Mr. Plum.[5] According to Savage, Francis Norton left no children, and there is no record of Clement Chaplin having left any either. Norton mentions a cousin John, by which he meant his nephew, and Chaplin's wife went back to England after Clement died, no children mentioned.

Helen Evertson Smith [6] summed up the Rev. Henry this way in 1900:

While the rule in New England pastorates was that the pastor was literally as well as figuratively the head of an obedient flock , which paid him all due deference, and followed his lead as sheep follow the piping of the shepherd, the pastors who successively essayed the charge of the church in Wethersfield were the unfortunate exceptions. In no sense could Mr. Smith have found his new pastorate a bed of roses. Besides the privations and hardships common to all pioneer pastors, there seems to have been a strong and most unusual element of turbulence in the membership of this wilderness church, for two preceding ministers had tried and failed to unite the members of the congregation sufficiently to secure a settlement, and the trouble did not immediately cease upon Mr. Smith's installation. Previous to or about the time of his settlement in Wethersfield the most prominent of the insurgents, under advice of the Rev. John

Davenport and others, had removed to Stamford; yet the restless spirits who were left found enough to say against Mr. Smith's ministry during the next few years. There is evidence tending to show that he may have been too liberal in his construction of doctrinal views, and inclined to too great charity in matters of personal conduct, to suit the more rigid among the townsmen. In at least one instance matters went so far that the pastor was brought before the General Court on charges the nature of which is not now apparent; but it is recorded that fines which for that day were very heavy were laid upon certain individuals "for preferring a list of grievances against Mr. Smith and failing to prove in the prosecution thereof." From references to this, which appear in manuscript of about a century after this date, referring to this trial as a thing still remembered, it would seem that Mr. Smith was opposed to severity in church discipline, and also to the importation into the Connecticut Colony of the bribe to hypocrisy which was offered by the law restricting to church-members the right of suffrage in town as well as church matters; and that he also preferred to believe an accused man to be innocent untiol he was proved guilty, and even then did not believe in proceeding to extremities until after every gentle means had been tried in vain.

One cause of animadversion is said to have been that Mr. Smith had advocated the separation of a wife from a drunken husband who had frightfully abused her and her children. This seems to have been thought by some members of the congregation to indicate great laxity of moral principle on the part of the pastor; but evidently the majority of the people were with him on these and other disputed points, and so were his friends, Mr. Thomas Hooker, the beloved pastor of the church at Hartford, and Mr. Warham of Windsor. Another complaint against Mr. Smith was that he refused to listen to those who brought him reports concerning alleged infractions of church discipline, on the ground that many of these things were matters which lay solely between a man and his Maker. In the end Mr. Smith carried the church with him, and when he died, in 1648, he was sincerely mourned even by those who at one time had "despitefully used" him.

Mr. Smith is said to have been "a scholarly man of gentle birth and breeding, a persuasive preacher and a loyal friend."

Henry Stiles intriguingly remarks that Clement Chaplin, Rev. Henry's chief calumniator. "was quite a large land-holder, and both he and Mr. Smith had lands allotted to them, on both sides of the River, in the general distribution of 1639." This brings to mind the extended debate among historians on the relationship between the spirituality and economic ambitions of Puritans, both in Old and New England. Did Clement by any chance have in mind getting hold of Henry's land if Smith could be drummed out of Wethersfield?

Rev. Smith appears to have left us no written sermons, nor theological disquisitions. It appears that he was primarily a pastor, not seriously interested in doctrinal disputation or scholarly elucidations of Puritan beliefs.

Reverend Alonzo Chapin says that Henry Smith **"died in 1648, grieved and wearied with the burdens of the world,"** which may be compared with Henry's son Samuel remembering **"ye sweetnesse & ye Charity of my firste Father."**

It appears that Rev. Henry had 8 children or so, of whom 3 or 4 were born in England of a first wife, name unknown, and 5 or 4 were born of a second wife Dorothy in New England, at least 4 of them in Wethersfield CT. Dorothy's last name may or may not of been Cotton (which tantalizingly reminds one of the famous Puritan minister, the Rev. John Cotton of Boston (1585-1652)). One of Henry's daughters by his first wife, Mary, married Samuel Hale, to whom I now turn.

The genealogist Donald Lines Jacobus looked into the English origins of Samuel Hale [7] and decided that his family, which lived in Watton at Stone, Hertfordshire, **"was one of the yeoman class and in comfortable circumstances."** In this period, a yeoman was a kind of farmer who held his own land. Three siblings in this family migrated to New England: Samuel, his brother Thomas, and his sister Martha. The brothers started out in Hartford CT, but are said to have been later among the founders of Norwalk CT, though neither of them remained there either. Thomas eventually settled in Charleston MA with his wife, who (I quote Jacobus) **"had been an apprentice girl, but the Rev. John Eliot assures us that they both lived ' well approved by the saints.' "** This is where I will leave Thomas and his wife. Martha's husband was Paul Peck, who was a deacon of the First Church in Hartford, which is where I will leave Martha and Paul.

Samuel Hale arrived in Hartford CT perhaps as early as 1634, and became one of its original proprietors, and as such was entitled to some land there. He was still there in 1639, at which time he owned at least one additional plot of land he was given for having served in the war against the Pequot Indians in 1636 and 1637. By 1643 he was living in Wethersfield. In the early 1650s, he became one of the founders of Norwalk CT, where he again obtained some land. In 1660, he returned to Wethersfield CT, to the part which became Glastonbury CT, presumably upon the occasion of marrying Mary Smith, whose father, as I've said, was minister there. Samuel and Mary took the former residence of Gov. Thomas Welles, who died in 1659. Rev. Alonzo Chapin remarked in 1853 about this place that: **"It may serve to throw light upon the conveniencies [sic] of those days, to mention that this house had no stairs leading into the chamber, the second story being reached by means of a ladder. His wife's name was Mary."** I don't know whether Rev. Chapin meant the conjunction of the mentions of the ladder and Samuel's wife's name to suggest something or not.

7. The Pequot War.

Alarmed colonists before the Pequot War

It appears that Samuel Hale was at least to some extent a land owner by occupation, although he was also a sometime soldier. In particular, he served under then Captain John Mason in the Pequot War. He may have participated in the notorious action in 1637 at what the English called Fort Mystick, on the Mystic River. The Pequot War was an engagement between Pequot Indians and the English, whose forces consisted of a Massachusetts force under the command of John Underhill, a Connecticut under the command of Mason, and a number of Mohegan (Mohican) and Narragansett Indian allies. Altogether there were about 90 English, 70 Mohegans and some smaller number of Narragansetts. Before the engagement at Fort Mystick, Mason sent 20 of his men home to guard their villages from Indian attacks. Whether Samuel Hale was among them, I don't know. If he was, then he was a part of Mason's forces at Fort Mystick. The number of Pequots at Fort Mystick was probably 6 or 7 hundred, of whom at least 150 were warriors. The majority of the other 450 or 550 appear to have been women, children and old men. All most all of the Pequots in the Fort were killed, most of them burned to death after Mason ordered that the combustible fort in which they were trapped be set afire.

Moral evaluations of what became known to many as the Fort Mystic massacre have been many, and continue to be made. Captain John Mason himself wrote an account some 30 years after the event in which he says:

Massacre at Mystick

The *Captain* [speaking of himself in the third person] also said, WE MUST BURN THEM [capitals in the original]; and immediately into the *Wigwam* where he had been before, brought out a Fire-Brand, and putting it into the Matts with which they were covered, set the *Wigwams* on Fire. Lieutenant *Thomas Bull* and *Nicholas Omsted* beholding, came up; and when it was thoroughly kindled, the *Indians* ran as Men most dreadfully Amazed. And indeed such a dreadful Terror did the ALMIGHTY let fall upon their Spirits, that they would fly from us and run into the very Flames, where many of them perished. [8]

"Thus," says Captain Mason of the Pequots trapped in the burning Fort Mystick, "were they now at their Wits End, who not many Hours before exalted themselves in their great Pride threatening and resolving the utter Ruin and Destruction of all the *English*, Exulting and Rejoycing with Songs and Dances: But GOD was above them, who laughed his Enemies and the Enemies of his People to Scorn, making them as a fiery Oven: Thus were the Stout Hearts spoiled, having slept their last Sleep, and none of the Men could find their Hands: Thus did the LORD judge among the Heathen, filling the Place with dead Bodies!" Some 7 Pequots were captured, and 7 escaped.

Capt. John Mason

Mason wrote that before the campaign which led to the Fort Mystick massacre, he was dubious about undertaking it. He says:

But Capt. *Mason* [speaking of himself] apprehending an exceeding great Hazard in so doing, for the Reasons fore mentioned, as also some other which I shall forbear to trouble you with, did therefore earnestly desire Mr. *Stone* that he would commend our Condition to the LORD, *that Night*, to direct how & in what manner we should demean our selves in that Respect; He being our *Chaplin* and lying aboard our *Pink*, the Captain on shoar. In the *Morning* very early Mr. *Stone* came ashoar to the Captain's Chamber, and told him, he had done as he had desired, and was fully satisfied to sail for *Narragansett*, which the *next Morning* we put in Execution." [9]

Cotton Mather says of him that on the breaking out of the Pequot war:

Mr. Stone it was who, attending the soldiers as Chaplain, kept their courage ever high and holy through pious mindfulness, — who went to pray with them as they sailed, as they marched, in fatigue, in pain, and during the perils of a mortal struggle."

Capt. John Underhill

Captain John Underhill, commander of the Massachusetts forces in the assault on Fort Mystick, wrote, in consideration of the possible immorality of incinerating women and children:

It may be demanded, Why should you be so furious (as some have said). Should not Christians have more mercy and compassion? But I would refer you to David's war. When a people is grown to such a height of blood, and sin against God and man, and all confederates in the action, there he hath no respect to persons, but harrows them, and saws them, and puts them to the sword, and the most terriblest death that may be. Sometimes the Scripture declareth women and children must perish with their parents. Sometimes the case alters, but we will not dispute it now. We had sufficient light from the word of God for our proceedings.

Underhill no doubt had in mind a number of incidents which followed on the murder by Indians of John Stone. [10] According to the historian Alfred Cave:

John Stone was a member of an influential and wealthy London family. A licensed privateer who had once scourged the Caribbean, he had most recently pursued a career as a smuggler. Stone was, as New England's Puritans described him, a drunkard, lecher, braggart, bully, and blasphemer. Adding to his unsavory reputation were rumors that he had resorted to cannibalism while shipwrecked during one of his privateering expeditions. But the captain was also a very skillful entrepreneur whose savoir faire had won the admiration of English, Spanish, Portuguese, and Dutch officials from Brazil to New Netherland. Some of those admirers had aided and abetted his smuggling activities. Stone counted among his intimate friends both the governor of Virginia, Sir John Harvey, and the director general of New Netherland, Wouter Van Twiller.

It appears that in murdering Stone, certain Indians were exercising their customary retribution, in the traditional manner, it is said, of Algonquians (of which the Pequots were a branch), for a murder of one of their sachems (leaders, or perhaps better, spokesmen) by some Dutch. I say *certain Indians*, because as the historian Francis Jennings has noted, the murder may not have been committed by Pequots at all, but by Western Niantics, who were at the time allies of the Pequots. In any case, to many of the Indians, Dutch and English undoubtedly appeared to be of one kind. This led to other atrocities on both sides, such as the killing of the trader John Oldham by Indians. (I mentioned him earlier as a first settler of Wethersfield CT). In this case the Indians involved appear to have been not Pequots, but Eastern Niantics, who were at the time allies of the Narragansetts (who were at the time at odds with the Pequots). But then to some of the English, Indians appeared to be of all of one kind.

The Puritans, exercising what they seem to have taken as a customary retribution for the killing of John Oldham, sent an expedition in 1636 against the Pequots under the command of John Endecott (or Endicott), who was instructed to kill all the occupants of Block Island, where numerous Pequots were located. Endecott and his men failed to eliminate many Pequots (they couldn't find them), although there was considerable burning of wigwams and recent summer harvests of corn.

The Pequots began to retaliate in kind. Shortly before Mason and Underhill undertook their mission to Fort Mystick, the Pequots attacked Wethersfield CT and killed 6 men, 3 women, 20 cows and 1 mare, and carried away 2 young women, the eldest about 16 years old. The girls were later released, apparently physically unharmed, apparently because the Pequots had asked them to make gunpowder for them, and were disappointed to learn that the girls didn't know how.

Battlefields of the Pequot War — Battles & Sites

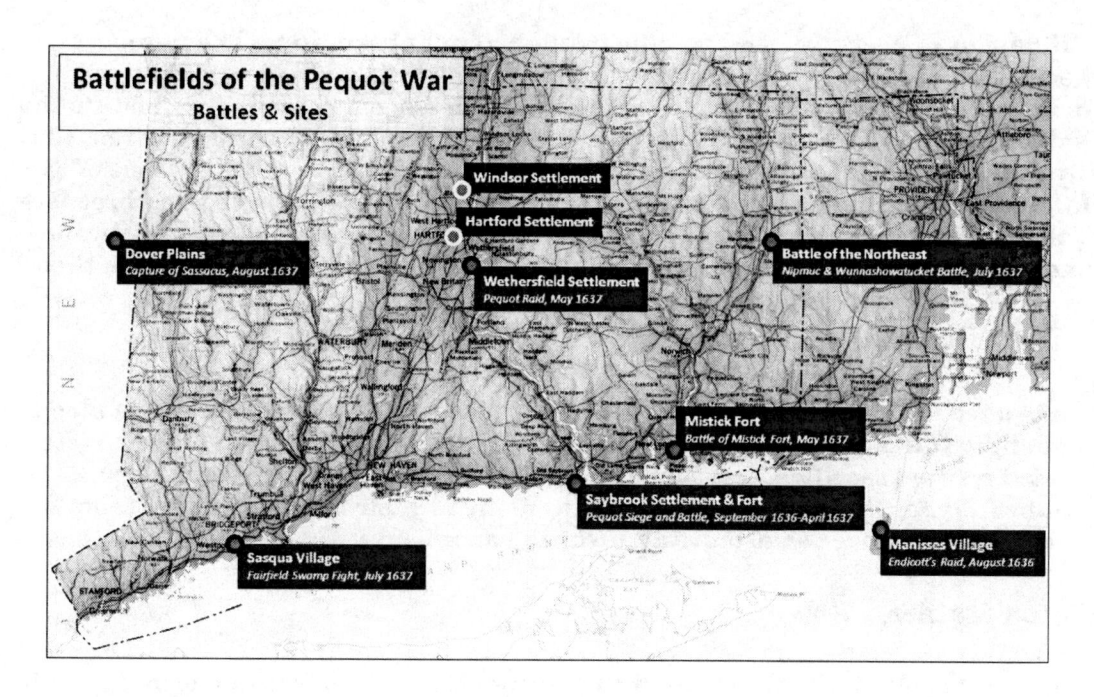

8. Evaluations.

John Winthrop, 1637:

The general defeat of the Pequods at Mistick happened the day after our general fast. ..... There was a day of thanksgiving kept in all the churches for the victory obtained against the Pequods, and for other mercies.

Philip Vincent, 1637:

An English man stept into a Wigwam and stooping for a fire-brand, an Indian was ready to knock out his braines. But he whipt out his sword and runne him into the belly, that his bowels followed. Then were the Wigwams set on fire, which so raged, that what therewith, what with the sword, in little more than an houre, betwixt three and foure hundred of them were killed, and of the English onely two, one of them by our owne Muskets, as is thought. For the Narragansets beset the Fort so close, that not one escaped. .....

They [the English immigrants] have overcome cold and hunger, are dispearsed securely in their Plantations sixty miles along the coast, and within the Land also along some small Creekes and Rivers, and are assured of their peace by killing the Barbarians, better than our English Virginians were by being killed by them. For having once terrified them, by severe execution of just revenge, they shall never heare of more harme from them, except (perhaps) the killing of a man or two at his worke, upon advantage, which their Centinels, and Corps du guards may easily prevent. Nay, they shall have those bruites their servants, their saves, either willingly or of necessity, and docible enough, if not obsequious. The numbers of the English amount to above thirty thousand, which (though none did augment them out of England) shall every day bee, doubtlesse, encreased, by a facultie that God hath given the Brittish Ilanders to beget and bring forth more children, than any other nation of the world. I could justifie what I say from the mouthes of the Hollanders and adjoyning Provinces, where they confesse (though good breeders of themselves) that never woman bore two children, nor yet had so many by one man, till the English and Scotch frequented their warres and married with them.

William Bradford, about 1650:

It was a fearful sight to see them thus frying in the fire and the streams of blood quenching the same, and horrible was the stink and scent thereof; but the victory seemed a sweet sacrifice, and they gave praise to God, who had wrought so wonderfully for them, as to enclose their enemy in their hands and give them so speedy a victory over so proud and insulting an enemy.

Cotton Mather, 1702:

It was on Friday, May 20, 1637, that this memorable action was performed; and it was rendred [sic] the more memorable by *this*, that the very night before what was now done, an hundred and fifty Indians were come from the other fort unto this, with a purpose to go out with all speed unto the destruction of some English town; whereas they were now suddenly destroy'd themselves; and in a little more than *one hour*, five or six hundred of these barbarians were dismissed from a world that was *burderned* with them; not more than seven or eight persons escaping of all that multitude.

Benjamin Trumbull, 1818:

It had been previously concluded not to burn the fort, but to destroy the enemy, and take the plunder; but the captain [Mason] afterwards found it the only expedient to obtain the victory, and save his men. Thus parents and children, the sannup [married man] and squaw, the old man and the babe, perished in promiscuous ruin.

John S. C. Abbott, 1857:

The heat [as the Pequot fort on the Mystic river burned] became so intense and the smoke so sothering that the English were compelled to retire outside of the fort. But they surrounded the flaming fortress, and every Indian who attempted to escape was shot. In one short hour the awful deed was accomplished. The whole interior of the fort was in ashes, and all the inmates were destroyed with the exception of seven only who escaped, and seven who were taken captives. The English knew that at a short distance from them there was another fort filled with Pequot warriors. It consequently was not sage to burden their little band with prisoners whom they could neither guard nor feed. They also wished to strike a blow which would appall the savages and prevent all future outrages. Death was, therefore, the doom of all.

John W. De Forest, 1852:

But of its moral features, what shall we say? What shall we say of this indiscriminate butchery of both sexes and all ages, allowing none or almost none to escape, but consigning nearly a whole community to a death of unsurpassed anguish and horror? ..... My own opinion of the burning of the Pequot fort is, that it was a piece of stern policy, mingled with something of revenge, from which floods of argument could not wash out a stain of cruelty.

John Gorham Palfrey, 1858:

When, for urgent reasons of public safety, it has been determined to take the desperate risk of sending scores of men into the field to encounter as many hundreds, and to be set upon, if they should be worsted, by as many thousands, the awful conditions of the case forbid being dainty about the means of winning a victory, or about using it in such a manner that the chance shall not have to be tried again. At all events, from the hour of that carnage, Connecticut was secure.

Henry Cabot Lodge, 1881:

The trouble with the Pequods belonged to Massachusetts and Plymouth; but while it was a peril to those colonies, it meant extermination and death to the settlers of Connecticut, where the savages were already murdering and burning on the outlying farms. The colonists faced the danger with stern Puritan courage. Their fighting men were mustered, and put under the command of John Mason, who led them against the stronghold of the Indians; and in the desperate assault upon the Pequod fort the men of Connecticut bore the heaviest share, and did more than any others to break the power of their formidable enemies, and give the land the peace of forty years.

Wethersfield and her Daughters Glastonbury, Rocky Hill, Newington, from 1634 to 1934, by Frances Wells Fox and Jared Butler Standish (Wethersfield), Lewis William Ripley (Glastonbury), Andrew Twaddle and William H. Dennis (Rocky Hill), Edwin Stanley Welles (Newington); 1934:

THE INDIAN MASSACRE, APRIL 23, 1637.

There is no Wethersfield record of this terrible event. Exaggerated rumors spread to the fort at the mouth of the river, and to the Massachusetts colony.

Mr. Sherman W. Adams. Wethersfield historian, considered Winthrop's account most correct. It was written about three weeks after the massacre. The blow came suddenly, probably in the early morning of that April day, as some of the settlers, men, women and children, were working in a "great field adjacent to the river" (the great Plain), between the river and the town. The Pequots had crept up the river in their log canoes under cover of the darkness, and had hidden behind trees and rushes, stealthy as shadows, until the workers were busy preparing and planting the land, probably in scattered groups. Then with a wild war whoop the savages pounced upon the unsuspecting victims. The Indians greatly outnumbered the whites. Three women and six men were killed. One party of Pequots carried off in great triumph, two girls, daughters of William Swayne. The Indians were wild with joy, as their canoes sped down the river. By the time they passed the fort, they had fastened smocks and shirts of their victims to poles and hoisted them in imitation of the sails of the white men's boats.

The girls were taken to Pequot (New London). Later they were redeemed and returned safely to their home. Tradition says the Indians had obtained possession of sixteen guns and they hoped to get the girls to show them how to make gun powder, but the girls were young and knew nothing of the art. The squaw of the sachem Mononotto took charge of the girls. She was kind, and no harm befell them. A short time later in the Pequot War this good squaw was captured. She was recognized by the English and she and the children were well taken care of by the orders of Governor Winthrop. She did not meet the fate of most of the squaws, who were sent as slaves to the West Indies.

Edward Eggleston, 1888 (in a textbook for schools):

The Pequot war in Connecticut grew out of the differences between the Dutch and English settlers. The English brought back the Indians whom the Pequot tribe had just driven away. The Pequots began the war by killing some English traders. ..... In 1637, John Mason, a trained soldier, at the head of a company of Connecticut men, with some from Massachusetts, marched into the Pequot country. At Mystic, Connecticut, just before daybreak, the Connecticut men surrounded the palisaded village of Sassacus, the dreaded Pequot chief. In the first onset Mason set the village on fire. A horrible slaughter followed." On the next page, Eggleston writes in a box: "Many of the white people sincerely desired to do the Indians good. ..... But even in trying to do the Indians good, the white men offended them. The chiefs and "medicine-men" of the Indians did not like to see their ancient customs treated with contempt, and their own influence destroyed by the new religion.

William Grimshaw, 1841 (in a textbook for schools):

By extending their settlements, the English became exposed to serious danger. The Indians around Massachusetts, being feeble and unwarlike, and having received from the early settlers what they deemed an equivalent for their lands, gave no indication of hostility: but Providence and Connecticut had to contend with nations more numerous and powerful. Among these, the most considerable were the Naragansets and the Pequods. The latter could bring into the field a thousand warriors; not inferior, in discipline and courage, to any Indians in America. Foreseeing that the extermination of their entire race must be the consequence of permitting Europeans to spread over the continent, they applied to the Naragansets; requesting them to forget their mutual animosities for a season, and co-operate in expelling a common enemy. But the latter, with a refinement in policy, similar to that which deluges with blood the numerous countries of the Christian world, perceived, in this, a favourable opportunity of weakening, if not of totally destroying, an ancient rival: instead, therefore, of acceding to this prudent offer, they discovered the hostile intention of their neighbours to the governor of Massachusetts, and entered into an alliance with the English against them.

"More exasperated than discouraged by this treachery, the Pequods took the field, plundered and burned remote settlements, and attacked fort Say Brook; from which, when driven off, they retired to places deemed inaccessible to an invading enemy. The troops of Connecticut were soon assembled, and ready for the field: but the march of those from Massachusetts was retarded by the most singular cause that ever influenced the operations of a modern army; reminding us of the superstitious Spartans, who, when solicited to join the Athenians in opposing the arms of Persia on the plains of Marathon, made answer, that it was an established law with them, not to begin a march before the full moon. When mustered, it being found that some of the officers and many of the private soldiers were "under a covenant of works," it was declared, that a blessing could neither be implored nor expected to accompany the arms of such unhallowed men. The alarm became general; and many arrangements were necessary, to cast out the unclean, and render this little band sufficiently pure to fight the battles of a people who entertained so high ideas of their own sanctity and importance.

Not waiting for their puerile allies [from English Massachusetts], the Connecticut troops, with the Naragansets, commanded by captain Mason, advanced against the enemy; who had posted themselves in the middle of a swamp, near the head of the river Mistic, and surrounded their camp with palisades. But they displayed more prudence in choosing their situation, than in guarding it from surprise. Their assailants reached the paling unperceived, and if a dog had not given the alarm, the Indians must have been massacred whilst asleep. In a moment, the warriors were in arms, and, raising the war cry, prepared to repel this formidable attack. Notwithstanding, however, that, like the defenders of the Roman capitol, they had been summoned by an instinctive guardian, they were not equally successful in overthrowing their invaders. A dreadful carnage ensued. Entering hastily by two winding passages, which had been left open, the English directed their guns towards the floors of the little huts, that were covered with their inhabitants asleep. Roused from their dreams by the unremitting discharges of musketry, if they came forth, they rushed against the surrounding swords; in they reached the palisades, and attempted to climb over, they were met by a shower of balls. Their crowded dwellings were soon in falmes: many, afraid to venture out, remained in the devouring fire; others, who had recoiled from the deadly weapons, rushed amidst the blaze, and shared their fate. In a few minutes, "five or six hundred lay gasping in their blood, or were silent in the arms of death." "The darkness of the forest," observes a New England author, "the blaze of the dwellings, the shrieks of the women and children, the yells of the friendly savages, presented a scene of sublimity and terror, indescribably dreadful." The Massachusetts' troops, under captain Stoughton, at length arrived, and in a few months the Pequods ceased to be a nation. Their very name was heard no more. Those who had been taken alive were sold as slaves, abroad, or reduced to servitude at home.

Francis Jennings, 1975:

As the first in a long series of New England's Indian wars, the "Pequot War" has been much written about by contemporaries as well as historians. Yet, more than three centuries after its occurrence, explanations of it are full of lacunae and contradictions. .....

"To get at the real motives for the Pequot conquest, we must attend to two major, inextricably interconnected events: the Pequots negotiation of a peace and friendship treaty with Massachusetts Bay in 1634 and the early colonization of the Connecticut Valley by Englishmen. ... ...

"At the center of the strife was the [Massachusetts] Bay magistrates' desire to control all colonizing in New England. ..... Now we must attend to a substantial group of orthodox Puritans led [into Connecticut] by the Reverend Thomas Hooker. ..... Connecticut was undeniably outside the limits set by Massachusetts's patent. That fact both attracted the dissenters and stimulated the magistrates to obstruct Hooker's plans to colonize Connecticut. .....

"In sum, Hooker's people intended to squat in territory that was already occupied by numerous Indians; that was claimed by Massachusetts, which had just acquired the preeminent Indian right to it; and that was further claimed by duly consituted agencies of both the Dutch and English nations. ... ...

"[By 1636] The whole region was in a most volatile condition. To preexisting Indian feuds the intruding English added their own quarrels and striving. The treaty between Massachusetts and the Pequots, which became also a peace between Pequots and Narragansetts, had brought a lull in violence and had opened the opportunity for orderly English expansion and orderly Pequot withdrawal. The treaty was a master stroke of Pequot diplomacy, recognizing the realities of power, retreating from untenable positions, and removing foreseeable causes of war. Ironically, however, its very existence stimulated and accelerated a competition between Massachusetts and Connecticut in which neither colony could succeed without first reducing the Pequots to overt subjection.

Howard S Russell, 1976:

When the Pilgrims arrived in 1620, not only did they find a large area of open, previously cultivated land at Plymouth and more on Cape Cod, but later noticed some of Boston Harbor's islands cleared from end to end and formerly cultivated. Their inhabitants, like Plymouth's, had been wiped out by a deadly sickness, three years after [Capt. John] Smith's visit [in 1614]. ..... Like those on Cape Cod and further north, the native Indians on the Rhode Island and Connecticut coasts who had escaped the plague were farming busily. Captain John Endecott, who fought some of them in 1636, commented on their many cornfields. He laid waste 200 acres of their corn on Block Island. In the Pequot War the next year, Captain John Mason of Connecticut, finding the Pequot village by the Pawcatuck River with its wigwams full of corn, loaded his ship with it before burning their wigwams.

Alden Vaughan, 1977:

That the war was a product of English land hunger and Pequot defense of its tribal territory, finds little documentation. It seems doubtful that in 1636 English settlers wanted land with which the Indians were unwilling to part. The Connecticut Valley tribes were welcoming the English and encouraging their settlement there. ..... The records clearly demonstrate that the bulk of the settlers proceeded upon the assumption that the Indian — heathen or not — had legal title to the lands upon which he lived, a title that could be changed only through the civilized conventions of sale and formal transfer. Only two instances exist in which the New Englanders acquired any substantial amounts of land from the Indians by means other than treaties. One was the Pequot War of 1637, the other King Philip's War of 1675-76; neither can reasonably be explained as campaigns for territorial expansion.

In seeking to identify the causes of the war and apportion responsibility for its outbreak, one must begin with the fact established by the testimony of all the whites and most Indians that the Pequots were blatantly and persistently provocative and aggressive. ..... On the other hand, it is undeniable that Puritan severity in the Endicott campaign provided the spark that set off the ultimate conflagration. Although the harshness of the Bay Colony's policy in the summer of 1636 is understandable, it cannot be excused.

While land as such was plainly not at issue, the Endicott expedition may well have represented something even more fundamental at stake here – the struggle between Puritans and Pequots for ultimate jurisdiction over the region both inhabited. The Puritans, determined to prevent Indian actions that might in any way threaten the New World Zion, had assumed through their governments responsibility for maintaining law and order among all inhabitants, Indian and white. ... ...

At bottom it was the English assumption of the right to discipline neighboring Indians that led to war in 1637. The Endicott expedition of 1636 was sent primarily to act as a police force, with orders to inflict punishment upon Block Island and obtain sureties of good behavior from the Pequots. The Pequots naturally resented the interference of Massachusetts in an area over which they had but recently acquired hegemony, and rejected the Bay Colony's assumption of the right to impose authority. The result was war.

Alden Vaughan, 1994:

The causes of the Pequot War are not easily unraveled. The reasons for the clash of the Puritan colonies, aided by the majority of the New England tribes, against the Pequots are legion: the restlessness of the River tribes under Pequot hegemony; the murder of ten or more Englishmen between 1634 and 1636, most notably Stone and Oldham; the severity of the Endicott expedition; the vicious Pequot raids that followed it; the urge for revenge that moved the Narragansetts and Mohegans; and the uncompromising attitudes of both Pequots and Puritans. From a mere recitation of the causes, one fact is clear: there was no "Indian side" to the story. The outlook of the Narragansetts, Mohegans, Massachusetts, and River tribes differed radically from that of the Pequots. And since most of the tribes of New England were on the white man's side, the Pequot war cannot accurately be described as an "Indian war" in the usual sense. This was no racial conflict between white man and red, no clash of disparate cultures or alien civilizations. What did propel New England into armed conflict was the attempt by the Puritan colonies -- supported by the bulk of the Indians -- to curb the militant Pequot tribe. The English had sought to live peacefully and equitably with their Indian neighbors; this they had been able to achieve until 1637. At the same time time the Puritans were determined to prevent criminal acts against English subjects. Besides their strong devotion to English law and Biblical injunction, there was their own safety to consider: it made little sense to escape the clutches of Bishop Laud only to fall prey to an Indian tomahawk. The Pequots, by contrast, wanted to maintain their recently acquired dominion over the Connecticut Valley and its inhabitants; they also seem to have had little respect for the lives of either Englishmen or Indians who were not under their dominion. Given this disparity of underlying intentions, it is not surprising that minor irritants swelled to unmanageable proportions.

Some of the blame for the war must fall on the Pequots, who, according to the testimony of all the whites and most of the Indians, were guilty of blatant and persistent aggression.

Richard Drinnon, 1980:

A short, quick step had thus taken the English from burning and spoiling the country to burning and spoiling some four hundred persons in little over an hour. ..... Though the Pequots were the first of the New England tribes to sense the genocidal intentions of the English and the implications of their different style of battle [involving killing of large numbers of non-combatants], the fury of the attack on their fort still was demoralizing.

Neal Salisbury, 1982:

The victory, though primarily a Connecticut accomplishment, was one with which all Puritans could identify. The rhetoric and imagery of the Pequot slaughter were deliberately reminiscent of the Old Testament, particularly of the Israelites "smiting" the Canaanites and driving them from the Promised Land. In 1637 this message was important.

Laurence Hauptmann, 1990:

What befell the Pequots in 1637 and afterward clearly fits the most widely accepted definition of genocide, one set by the United Nations Convention on Genocide in 1948. ..... Modern Pequots use this tragedy to overcome tragedy. They see their present-day successes as the long culmination of holding actions and survival strategies developed over the centuries. The War of 1637 is thus indelibly marked in the contemporary Pequot's psyche and has influenced nearly every phase of the tribal renaissance over the past decade and a half. Moreover, Pequots can hardly escape their past even if they try, since their reservations date from the mid-1660s and the site of the Mystic Fort is only ten miles down the road from the reservation.

Alfred Cave, 1996:

Celebration of victory over Indians as the triumph of light over darkness, civilization over savagery, for many generations our central historical myth, finds its earliest full expression in the contemporary chronicles and histories of this little war. The myth from its inception was grounded in a distorted conception of Indian character and behavior. The Pequot War was not waged in response to tangible acts of aggression. It cannot be understood as a rational response to a real threat to English security. It was, however, the expression of an assumption central to Puritan Indian policy. Puritan magistrates were persuaded that from time to time violent reprisals against recalcitrant savages would be necessary to make the frontier sage for the people of God. The campaign against the Pequots was driven by the same assumption that had impelled Plymouth to massacre Indians suspected of plotting against them at Wessagusett in 1623. The incineration of Pequots at Fort Mystic served the same symbolic purpose as the impalement of Wituwamet's head on Plymouth's blockhouse. Both were intended to intimidate potential enemies and to remind the Saints that they lived in daily peril of massacre at the hands of Satan's minions.

Robert Fuller, 1995:

In his lengthy history of the American colonies, *Magnalia Christi Americana*, Cotton Mather explained that Satan had beaten them to the New World and had already laid the traps with which he intended to snare his opponents. The Native Americans, Mather surmised, were Satan's first line of defence against the forces of righteousness: "Though we know not when or how these Indians first became inhabitants of this mighty continent, yet we may guess that probably the devil decoyed these miserable savages hither in hopes that the gospel of the Lord Jesus Christ would never come here to destroy or disturbe his absolute empire over them." [1702] ... ...

The Puritans' proclivity for demonizing their enemies served an even more important ideological function when it became necessary to murder the Native Americans wholesale. For a community that had conceived of itself as dedicated to the gospel of love, the widescale slaughter of Indians posed serious questions about the Puritans' character and moral resolve. Knowing that their adversaries were in league with Satan helped ease the consciences of God's chosen people. Within weeks of arriving on the shores of Plymouth, the Pilgrims had been forced of necessity to raid Indian storage bins for corn and native crafts. Violent skirmishes broke out from time to time, leading up to the Pequot War of 1637 in which the Puritans killed more than five hundred native men, women, and children in a single battle.

See: http://ancientlights.org/mysticfiasco.html   (accessed Jul 2013)

Probably it is not possible to estimate reliably how many of the Puritans engaged in the Pequot War were motivated by a conscious desire to corner trade or to acquire land; nor how many by an intention to exert authority over the Indians whether in the name of law or order or for other purposes; nor how many by the belief that Indians were in league with the Devil or at any rate used by Satan for his purposes; nor how many by a desire to protect their families or to share danger with their comrades; nor how many by unanalyzed fear of Indians once some of them had begun to fight Europeans in earnest; nor how many by some combination of these or by still other emotions or reasons or rationalizations. Nor, given the conditions that prevailed at the battle site, will it be easy for many combat veterans to condemn Captain Mason unqualifiedly for setting on fire the Pequot fort on the Mystic River, however much the veterans might be moved by natural feelings common to a large part of humankind that the action was unduly and perhaps inexcusably cruel.

Whether or not Samuel Hale was present at the Fort Mystick operation, he did serve under Mason in the overall campaign, which continued for some time after the immolation at Mystick, and resulted in more slaughter of Pequots. It was at one time widely believed that in these years, the Pequot tribe was totally exterminated. Early on, the Connecticut General Assembly declared that the name Pequot had become extinct (some captives were taken by other tribes as "vassals" or sent to Bermuda as slaves), and that no survivors should carry that name. In Herman Melville's *Moby Dick*, published in 1851, *Pequod*, a variant of Pequot, is the name of the ill-fated ship commanded by Captain Ahab. "***Pequod*, you will no doubt remember,**" says Melville, "**was the name of a celebrated Indian tribe of Massachusetts Indians, now extinct as the ancient Medes.**"

Yet scattered individual Pequots did survive, and the name lived on. In 1983 both houses of the U. S. Congress unanimously approved a Pequot claim for $900,000 to buy 800 acres to establish their own reservation. U. S. President Ronald Reagan vetoed the claim on the grounds that this was "**too much to pay**" these improbable survivors, as the historian Richard Drinnon put it. In fact, though (as reported by Jack Campisi), the White House agreed to reconsider the bill if certain conditions were met, notably that the state of Connecticut put up more money toward the $900,000, and that the Pequots submit a formal request for official recognition by the U.S. government. The legislation was reintroduced in an amended form, and the new version was passed in October of 1983. The federal government acknowledged that the Pequots still exist, after all.

From the *U. S. News & World Report* for March 15, 1993:

Off the reservation. The Federal Election Commission last week released a list of individuals and organizations that donated at least $100,000 in 'soft money' to the major political parties during the 1992 presidential campaign. The most unexpected entry on the list: the Mashantucket Pequot tribe of Connecticut, which gave $100,000 to the Democratic National Committee. A spokesman for the 250-member tribe — which runs a $500 million-a-year gambling casino on its reservation outside New London [CT] — explained that the contribution was made to the Democrats because they 'recognize the need for Native Americans to have better housing and education.' But sources off the 1,800-acre reservation say that the tribe may have been making one of the best bets in American politics: gambling on a prospective winner. The tribe wants to expand its booming casino operation into a full-service resort and would like to buy 1,200 nearby acres formerly used as a Boy Scout camp. However, before it can expand the reservation, the Mashantucket Pequot tribe needs approval from the Bureay of Indian Affairs, a unit of the Interior Department, which is now run by Bruce Babbitt, who, of course, is a Democrat.[11]

Mrs. Lydia Huntley Sigourney of Connecticut wrote in her poem of 1841:

Forgotten race, farewell! Your haunts we tread;
Our mighty rivers speak your words of yore;
Our mountains wear them on their misty head;
Our sounding cataracts hurl them to the shore:
But on the lake your flashing oar is still;
Hushed is your hunter's cry on dale and hill;
Your arrow stays the eagle's flight no more;
And ye, like troubled shadows, sink to rest
In unremembered tombs, unpitied and unblessed.
....
It is not meet thy name should moulder in the grave.

9. Samuel Hale after the Pequot War.

During the time of the Pequot War, Samuel Hale was in his early twenties and unmarried. His wedding to Mary Smith took place in 1642/43, and together they had 9 children. He acquired a lot of land in Connecticut, and served several times as a Deputy to the Connecticut General Court, as a selectman for Wethersfield, was an original proprietor of Hartford and a founder of Norwalk, and served on numerous juries. Jacobus and Waterman note in this connection that "On 4 Dec. 1645, he was fined twenty nobles "**for his mysdemeanor by excesse in drinkeing,**" but was again called for jury duty, 1 Oct. 1646." Samuel died in Glastonbury CT, 9 Nov 1693, at the age of 78. I don't have the Mary's date of death, but it appears Samuel was married a second time to Phebe (Bracy)(Dickinson) Rose. They had no children, and Phebe is not mentioned in Samuel's will, even though she is reported to have died in 1710/11, well after Samuel.

Here is Samuel's will, taken from Donald Lines Jacobus and Edgar Francis Waterman, *Hale, House and Related Families, Mainly of the Connecticut River Valley,* Hartford, CT (Connecticut Historical Society) 1952:

Glassonbury December the twenty sixt one thousand sixe hundred and ninetie two—

I Samll Hale senir being of perfect understanding and memorie and perceiving in myself the symptoms of mortality and knowing that all flesh must yield to death when God shall call and being minded to sett things in order, doe make and declare this my last will and testamt in maner and form following, hereby revoking and annulling all former and other will and wills testament and testaments heretofore by me made and declared either by word or writing and this to be taken onely for my last will and testamt and no other: And first and principally I commend my soul into the hands of almight god, in christ Jesus my merciful creator and redeemer, my body to the earth from whence it was taken, to be buried in such decent and christian like manner as to my executrs hereafter by me named shall seem meet and convenient—And for the setling of my temporall estate and such goods and Chattells as god of his meer bounty farre above my desert hath given to me, I doe give and dispose of the same in manner and forme following. And first my will is that all my debts whatsoever that I owe either in lawe or conscience to any prson or persons whatsoever be well and truely paid or ordained to be paid within convenient time after my decease, my debts and funerall expenses being discharged. As I have formerly given to my beloved sons Samuel, John, Thomas, and Benezer considerable portions in lands I doe now give and bequeath to my beloved son Samuel my Muskett and my two horsbrands. Item I give and bequeath to my beloved son John a pair of shoes the best pair of my wearing shoes that I shall leave at my decease. Item I give and bequeath to my son Benezer all my right and title to threscore acrs of land granted to me by the Generall Court for my service in the pequot warre: my said right and title to stand as good and firm to him to all Intents and purposes and to his heirs for ever as it

should or might have done to me and to my heirs for ever. I doe also give and bequeath to my said Beloved son Benezer my great bible and all the rest of my books except one of Mr Dikes his works formerly given to my daughter in law Naomi. Item I give and bequeath to my beloved son Thomas all my Cask and barls whatsoever that have been used to hold Corn. Item I give and bequeath to my beloved Daughters Marie Rebeccah and Dorothie to each of them one of my greatest peauter platters. And to my said daughter Rebeccah I also give my three pint peauter pot. Item I give and bequeath to my beloved Grandchildren John Hale and Thomas Hale the sons of my son John Hale, all my Interest in that tract of land lying on the east side of the said town of Glassenbury and being sixemiles in length and five in breadth, to have and to hold all my right and Interest in the said tract of land to them and their heirs for ever: And my will is that if either of my said grandchildren shall happen to dye before me, or under age: that then all my right and Interest in the said tract of land shall be to the serviver and his heirs for ever. Item I give and bequeath to my said grandchild Thomas Hale my great chest and all my wearing Clothes, a sword, a great square glasse a pint glasse and a half pint glasse also all my axes hoes beetle rings and wedges also a horse or mare my sadle and handsaw and powder flask: and a hive of bees. Item I give and bequeath to my grandchild Abigail Beniamin all my bedsteds beds and bedding and all the linnen that I shall leave at my decease. Also 1 cowe and 1 mare and my great brass Kettle, my firepan tongs trammel frying pan and warming pan. Also one peauter platter and bason with my name on them, and a small bason, an Iron pot a quart skillet and a pint skillet, her grandmothers chest and all her grandmothers linnen and woollen (which I formerly Inhuaged to her that she should have them) Also I give and bequeath to my said grandchild Abigail, my gridiron, chamber pot, two great chairs and a little one and all my wooden bowles platters dishes and spoons, a new poudering tub with the flesh I shall leave in it at my decease also my boxiron and heaters. Also my brass chafing dish, stewpan lid, lamp, and candlestick, two wheels two apir of Kards and Kneeding trough or bowl, my spit and sieve, also my pannel pillion and bridle scaels two pound weight 1 pound weight, half pound weight and 1 hive of bees I give to my said grandchild abigail. Also I give to her my half bushel my bear barrel a small milk keeler and two pails. And I doe appoint and constitute my forementioned beloved sons Samll Hale and Thomas Hale executrs of this my last will and Testament. In Witness thereof I have hereunto sett to my hand the day and year above written—Signed and delivered in the presence of us

Eleazr Kimberly	his
Samuel Emons	Samuel + Hale senr
	mark

Eleazar Kimberly and samll Emons personally appearing this sixt day of december 1693 gave their severall respective testimonies upon oath before me that the above written Instrument was signed and delivered by Samll Hale senr the testator therein mentioned as his last will and testament I say before me

John Chester: Comisser

Glassenbury Novembr 13: 1693 An Inventorie of the estate of Samll Hale senr deceased the 9th of this Instant—taken by us Eleazr Kimberly and Joseph Hill select men:

	lb s d
Impr His apparell	08 00 00
Item: bedsteads bedds and bedding	10 00 00
Item: gun sword and belt and flash	02 00 00
Item: pewter platters pots and basons	01 10 00
Item: Brasse and Iron vessels	03 00 00
Item: Books	01 00 00
Chests 1lb: wooden vessells and sieve 10s	01 10 00
Item: frying pan spitt 10s: hour glasse looking glasse and brush 4s—all	00 14 00
Item: beetle rings wedges axes and other Iron implements	01 10 00
Item: Trammel tongs fire pan smoothing Iron and heaters	01 00 00
Item: Sadle pannell and bridle	00 10 00
Item: Scaols and weights 3s Coopers ware 20s	01 03 00
Item: provision for the familie 15s: baggs 4s	00 19 00
Item: Corn in the Chamber and in the barn	14 00 00
Item: hops 10s: tobacco 15s: hay 3lb	04 05 00
Item: flaxe 1lb 10s: 2 cowes 8lb 1 Calf 15s	10 05 00
Item: 2 swine 1lb: 10s i horse 2 mares 2 Colts 9lb	10 10 00
Item: 24 pound of yarn	02 08 00
Item: Glasse bottles baskets and pumpions	00 08 00
Item: 2 brand Irons 5s 2 chairs and wheels 8s i hive of bees 12s	01 05 00
Item: salt	00 04 00
[total]	74 01 00

[Signed by Eleazr Kimberly and Joseph Hills.]

One of the children of Samuel Hale and Mary (Smith) Hale, born 7 Feb 1644/45, was Samuel Hale, Jr, to whom I now turn.

10. Samuel Hale, Jr., Justice of the Peace

Samuel Hale, the son of Samuel Hale, was known in later life as Lieutenant Samuel Hale (though he was known for a long time as Sergeant Hale), and I will refer to him here as Lt. Samuel to distinguish him from his father. He was born in 1645 (new style) in Wethersfield, and died in Glastonbury (which by then had broken off from Wethersfield) in 1711, aged 67 years. He appears to have chiefly worked as a soldier, town and colony official, and presumably farmer, aside from marrying twice, and contributing to raising the consequent families.

His first wife was Ruth Edwards, daughter of Thomas Edwards and someone whose name is unknown to me. Lt. Samuel married Ruth in 1670. Ruth died in 1682, aged 30 years, after giving birth to 5 children. His second wife was Mary Welles, daughter of Samuel and Elizabeth (Hollister) Welles, and granddaughter of Thomas and Alice (Tomes) Welles. Thomas was a prominent citizen of Hartford CT, the first treasurer of the Connecticut colony, and later governor. He was one of the officials who voted to wage war on the Pequots in 1636.[12]

Lt. Samuel was for many years a justice of the peace in Glastonbury. His epitaph reads: **"Here lieth inhumed the body of Mr. Samuel Hale, Esq., of late one of Her Majestie's Justices of the Peace, who d. on the 18th day of Nov'r Anno Dom. 1711, and in the 67th year of his age."** He also served for many years on the general court of the colony, and was for some time the captain of the local militia, or as it was called then, the *train band*.

Lt. Samuel Hale acquired before 1688 some land which had been owned by his grandfather Rev. Henry Smith. He also acquired in 1701 some land which had once belonged to Clement Chaplin, Henry Smith's cantankerous adversary, and then to Josiah Walcott. Actually, the Rev. Alonzo Chapin reported in 1853 that Lt. Samuel acquired 2/3 of the land. When the land came up for the sale, Lt. Samuel consulted with his pastor Rev. Timothy Stevens about the advisability of buying it. According to Rev. Alonzo, "**Mr. Stevens deeming it an excellent bargain on the terms offered, advised the purchase, only insisting that he should be permitted to come in with Mr. Hale and take one-third of it.**" Rev. Alonzo also reports that at one time Lt. Samuel was a member of the Glastonbury School Society, which I take it was what now would be called a school board.

11. Wethersfield and her Daughters,

I wish I could say more about Lt. Samuel Hale's two wives beyond their names and the names and dates of their children, but the records of the time known to me reveal nothing more of them. One can get some idea of what their lives were like from general descriptions like the following:

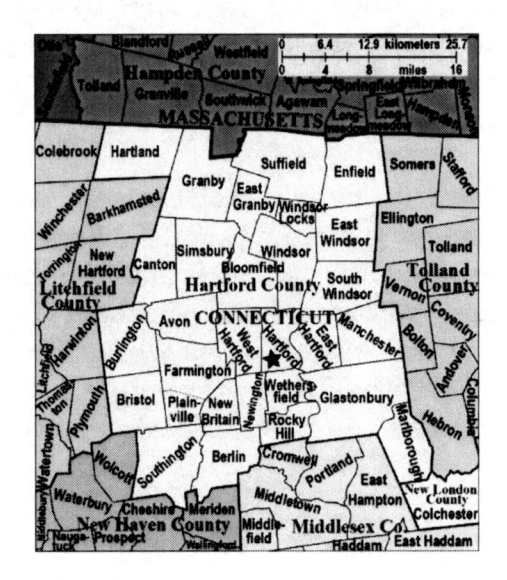

Wethersfield and her Daughters: Glastonbury, Rocky Hill, Newington, from 1634 to 1934, by Frances Wells Fox and Jared Butler Standish (Wethersfield), Lewis William Ripley (Glastonbury), Andrew Twaddle and William H. Dennis (Rocky Hill), Edwin Stanley Welles (Newington), c. 1934:

All the people were English and had their own ideas as to a town and colony government, which differed from those of Winthrop in Massachusetts. At a meeting of the General Court in February 1636, the town was given the name of Wethersfield, probably at the suggestion of some one from old Wethersfield in England. They soon built substantial houses, with great fireplaces, for wood was easy to procure. There was very little furniture. Stools, benches, and forms were used and a little later the high back settle by the fireplace.

They had no tea, coffee or potatoes, and very little sugar, but after trade began with the West Indies sugar and molasses were more plentiful. Bees were valued highly. The water in the Great River was unpolluted. In the early spring the river teemed with shad, salmon and alewives. It was customary to put a shad or a couple of alewives in a hill of corn for fertilizer. Game was abundant in the woods- -- wild ducks, geese and turkeys. The settlers brought pigs and a few goats as well as cattle. The pigs were allowed to run at large. When Nathaniel Foote [13] died in 1644 his "hoggs" were valued at more than his horses. Leonard Chester left "Hoggs" in his estate in 1648. There were no sheep until after the wolves had been partially

exterminated. Both the town and colony paid a bounty on their heads; this reduced the numbers in a few years ... ...

At one time there was a tavern to welcome the thirsty wanderer of the sea, and a school in a private house for the little girls of the neighborhood, where they were taught to read and spell, and to sew "a fine seam". One little girl made a shirt for her brother which was treasured in the family for many years. They were also taught to make their curtsy to the minister when he called and never to tell a lie.

Early in the nineteenth century Sophia Woodhouse manufactured straw bonnets at her home. She used the grass growing in the "Flats" of the Common, and perfected a process of making fine Leghorn bonnets.

Rev. Alonzo B. Chapin, D.D., 1853:

The increase of the population [in Glastonbury] seems to have been more rapid at this period, than could have been expected. In 1693, we have seen there were thirty-four householders, and it will appear from documents given below, that in 1714, there were sixty-four resident tax payers, and probably householders. In 1723, the number had increased to one hundred and eighteen. As late as 1757, the number was one hundred and ninety-nine. This increase of population was so rapid, that the meeting-house which had been built in 1693, was found too small to accommodate the people as early as 1706, and it was accordingly voted to enlarge the same "by galleries or lean-tos, as the committee should judge most expedient." What order was first observed in regard to seats in the meeting-house, does not appear; but in 1712, a committee was appointed "to seat the meeting-house," and a vote passed that persons not sitting in the seats assigned by the committee, should pay "a fine of five shills a year." The committee finding the subject attended with very great difficulty, declined going through with the work; in consequence of which it is said there had been "great disorders on Sabbath days, and other days of Public Worship," whereupon a new committee was appointed, and persons refusing to sit in the seats assigned them were fined "fifteen shillings a month." What kind of seats were employed in the meeting-house is nowhere mentioned, but that they were not pews, is evident from a vote passed Dec., 1717, permitting Thomas Kimberly, and Richard Goodrich "to build each of them a pue [sic] in the meeting-house."

Mary Jeanne Anderson Jones, 1968:

In their dress and habits the Puritans were not radical. They wore bright colors and silver buttons on their waistcoats and dresses, as long as they were obtainable. But they also dressed in leather and homespun on working days. These were far more appropriate to their stations than would have been the lace and silks adorned with expensive jewelry found at Court. Only the ministers wore black habitually. Children played with dolls and toys, though simple ones, of course. The Puritans frowned on secular music and art, but not on beauty in itself. Wine and beer formed an important element in their daily diet, but inebriation they abhorred. Their morals were reasonable, contrary to popular conception, and not Victorian. Love in the home was a vital part of the marriage.

John Demos, 1986:

And what of women ..... ? Along with men -- perhaps *more* than men -- women in mid-life knew the power of parenthood. A New England "goodwife" in her forties and fifties would likely preside over a household of ten or a dozen; not for her the "empty nest," either in actuality or in prospect -- quite the contrary. Her relation to her daughters (and maidservants "bound over" from elsewhere) was especially encompassing; to them she stood as ruler, tutor, example, protectress, all in one. Her duties were manifold, her skills indispensable. Gardening, cooking, dairying, textile production: thus the leading forms of specifically female labor, each one in itself subdivided into numerous smaller operations. "In the agricultural towns and villages of early New England," one scholar has written, "women were the ones whose knowledge guided the key transformation of nature into culture." Men "broke" the raw materials of Nature (e.g. by cultivating and harvesting a variety of animal and vegetable products), while women "improved" these same materials (through processing and preparing them for human consumption).

This sounds like a "domestic" definition of women's lives; and so indeed it was. Yet with some regularity women stepped out into roles and activities beyond the home-hearth. They entered the local economy, especially in marketing herbs, cheeses, cloth, and other products of their own hand. They practiced a traditional "doctoring," sometimes in direct competition with male physicians. (One branch of medicine belonged exclusively to women: childbirth was for female hands and eyes only, with midwives officially in charge.) They assisted their menfolk in running taverns, inns, and small shops. At least occasionally they went into court as "attorneys" for temporarily absent husbands. There is enough evidence here for one scholar to have invented the term "deputy husband" as a way of describing the full range of women's responsibilities in early New England.

Bruce Daniels, 1995:

No New England colony ever passed a general statute forbidding dancing, but colony and local laws hedged it about with extreme restrictions. A controversy over the probity of dancing surfaced in Salem [MA] in 1635. The congregation's young minister, Richard Levett, asked Boston's leading theologian, John Cotton, for guidance. Cotton replied that one should not automatically condemn all dancing. He cited a passage in Exodus that supported dance "lending to the praise of ... God." Cotton, continued, however, that this did not include "lascivious dancing to wanton ditties, and amourous gestures and wanton dalliances ... [which] I would bear witness as a great *flabella Libidinis*" [fanning of sexual desire]. And herein lay the problem: at its worst, dancing was thought to incite adultery and fornication. Being particularly popular everywhere with women, dancing allegedly caused them to lower their guard against attacks on their chastity. Hence "lascivious dancing," which authorities defined as any dancing that allowed men and women to touch or hold each other, was forbidden, as was any association between alcohol and dancing.

Rev. Samuel Peters', LL. D., 1781:

Weathersfield [sic] is four miles from Hertford [sic], and more compact than any town in the colony. The meeting-house is of brick, with a steeple, bell, and clock. The inhabitants say it is much larger than Solomon's Temple. The township is ten miles square; parishes four. The people are more gay than polite, and more superstitious than religious. This town raises more onions than are consumed in all New-England. It is a rule with parents to buy annually a silk gown for each daughter above seven years old, till she is married. The young beauty is obliged, in return, to weed a patch of onions with their own hands; which she performs in the cool of the morning, before she dresses the beefsteak. This laudable and healthy custom is ridiculed by the ladies of other towns, who idle away their mornings in bed, or in gathering the pink, or catching the butterfly, to ornament their toilets; while the gentlemen, far and near, forget not the Weathersfield ladies' silken industry. ..... The women of Connecticut are strictly virtuous, and to be compared to the prude rather than the European polite lady. They are not permitted to read plays; cannot converse about whist, quadrille, or operas, but will freely talk upon the subject of history, geography, and mathematics. They are great casuists and polemical divines; and I have known not a few of them so well skilled in Greek and Latin as often to put to the blush learned gentlemen. .....

Notwithstanding the modesty of the females is such that it would be accounted the greatest rudeness for a gentleman to speak, before a lady, of a garter, knee, or leg, yet it is thought but a piece of civility to ask her to bundle – a custom as old as the first settlement in 1634. It is certainly innocent, virtuous, and prudent, or the puritans would not have permitted it to prevail among their offspring, for whom, in general, they would suffer crucifixion. Children brought up with the chastest ideas, with so much religion as to believe that the omniscient God sees them in the dark, and that angels guard them when absent from their parents, will not – nay, cannot – act a wicked thing. People who are influenced more by lust than a serious faith in God, who is too pure to behold iniquity with approbation, ought never to bundle. ..... The Indians, who had this method of courtship when the English arrived among them in 1634, are the most chaste set of people in the world. ..... I am no advocate for temptation, yet must say that bundling has prevailed 160 years in New-England, and, I verily believe, with ten times more chastity than the sitting on a sofa.

12. Gov. Thomas Welles and the Fundamental Orders

Mary Welles, second wife of Samuel Hale, Jr., was born at Glastonbury CT in 1666, and died there in 1714/15, aged 48. Her parents were Samuel Welles (c1628 - 1675) and Elizabeth Hollister who was born in Wethersfield CT in 1640 and whose date of death I don't know. Samuel was married previously to Ruth Edwards, but Mary was the mother of all his children.

Mary's mother, Elizabeth Hollister, is to me another mostly unknown person. Elizabeth and her husband Samuel Welles had six children, born between 1660 and 1670. Writing about Elizabeth in 1886, Lafayette Wallace Case says: "**She married Samuel Welles, son of Gov. Thomas Welles of the Connecticut Colony, in 1659. She died, and he married 2d, Hannah, daughter of George Lamberton of New Haven; no children by the second marriage.**" Just *she died*, no more. Incidentally, after Samuel Welles died, his widow Hannah married John Allyn of Hartford. It appears that there was a lot of visiting going on, back and forth between Wethersfield, Glastonbury, Hartford and New Haven. Hannah's father George Lamberton was captain of the once locally famous *Phantom Ship*, lost at sea in 1646, or more precisely about Capt. Nathaniel Turner, who perished with Capt. Lamberton, and Nathaniel's daughter Rebecca, who married Thomas Mix of New Haven.[14] Henry Wadsworth Longfellow wrote a poem about this:

The Phantom Ship

In Mather's Magnalia Christi,
  Of the old colonial time,
May be found in prose the legend
  That is here set down in rhyme.

A ship sailed from New Haven,
  And the keen and frosty airs,
That filled her sails at parting,
  Were heavy with good men's prayers.

"O Lord! if it be thy pleasure"—
  Thus prayed the old divine—
"To bury our friends in the ocean,
  Take them, for they are thine!"

But Master Lamberton muttered,
  And under his breath said he,
This ship is so crank and walty
  I fear our grave she will be!"

And the ships that came from England,
   When the winter months were gone,
Brought no tidings of this vessel
   Nor of Master Lamberton.

This put the people to praying
   That the Lord would let them hear
What in his greater wisdom
   He had done with friends so dear.

And at last their prayers were answered:—
   It was in the month of June,
An hour before the sunset
   Of a windy afternoon,

When, steadily steering landward,
   A ship was seen below,
And they knew it was Lamberton, Master,
   Who sailed so long ago.

On she came, with a cloud of canvas,
   Right against the wind that blew,
Until the eye could distinguish
   The faces of the crew.

Then fell her straining topmasts,
   Hanging tangled in the shrouds,
And her sails were loosened and lifted,
   And blown away like clouds.

And the masts, with all their rigging,
   Fell slowly, one by one,
And the hulk dilated and vanished,
   As a sea-mist in the sun!

And the people who saw this marvel
   Each said unto his friend,
That this was the mould of their vessel,
   And thus her tragic end.

And the pastor of the village
   Gave thanks to God in prayer,
That, to quiet their troubled spirits,
He had sent this Ship of Air.

Footnote by Longfellow:

A detailed account of this "apparition of a Ship in the Air" is given by Cotton Mather in his Magnalia Christi, Book I, Ch. VI. It is contained in a letter from the Rev. James Pierpont, Pastor of New Haven. To this account Mather adds these words:—

"Reader, there being yet living so many credible gentlemen, that were eye-witnesses of this wonderful things, I venture to publish it for a thing as undoubted as 't is wonderful."

Rollin G Osterweis says, 1953:

Perhaps the incident is less a legend than the poet believed. Even the most critical historian must admit that the world of imagination loomed large in the thoughts of the Puritan colonist. Thomas J Wertenbaker has suggested, in connection with this story of the Phantom Ship, that "the God of seventeen-century New England was a God of dramatic revelations." [*The First Americans, 1607-1690*, 1927] Any deviation from the known outline of nature was taken as a "sign from heaven." In such a climate of opinion, a weird cloud formation, a storm, and a rainbow could appear convincingly significant. And with a John Davenport on hand to interpret the "sign from Heaven," the miracle need not have stemmed entirely from the literary inventions of a later day.

Viewed against the general background of the colony's history, the loss of the Lamberton ship marked one more setback to the ambitions of the merchant adventurers. The attempt to establish direct trade with England took place after the Delaware experiment appeared destined to fail. Winthrop's comments on the ill-fated voyage intimate the almost desperate attitude of those who arranged it. Unwilling to wait for the frozen harbor to thaw, the eager inhabitants cut through three miles of ice in order to send their ship out to sea. The cargo of wheat, West India hides, and beaver represented a value of more than L5000, and the ship's passenger list included Mr. Gregson and another magistrate, Captain Turner, Mrs. Goodyear, and seven or eight additional figures of importance. One gets the impression of a daring gamble designed to reverse a series of economic disappointments. The loss of the "Great Shippe" weakened the financial structure of the colony and thus played a significant part in its subsequent decline.
...... [from a chronology]:
1647 Mr. Gregson, Captain Turner, and several other prominent New Haveners leave New Haven in January for a trading voyage to London in "The Great Shippe." They are never heard from again.

Mary's father, Capt. Samuel Welles, was a son of Thomas Welles and Alice Tomes, brought by them from England, born according to William Richard Cutter, in Rothwell, Northamptonshire, England, about 1630. It appears that although Samuel was a captain, he led a relatively peaceful life, sandwiched between the two Puritan-Indian wars, the Pequot War of 1636-1637 and King Philip's War of 1675-1677. He was, though, a member of the War Council in

July of 1675. Samuel died at Wethersfield Ct on 15 July 1675. King Philip's War began in earnest in the latter part of June, 1675.

Samuel held a number of official town positions in Wethersfield, and spent the last ten years of his life as Commissioner (or Justice) for Wethersfield. He was an officer in the Train Band (the local militia) from 1658 to 1670. That his relationship with Indians was relatively peaceful may be seen from the following agreement, transmitted by Marjorie Grant McNulty in 1970. She says:

The town we now know as Glastonbury had its beginnings in 1636, when the Wethersfield proprietors bought from the sachem. Sowheag. a large tract of land measuring six miles west of the river, three miles east, and six miles from the north to south. No record of an Indian deed to the tract, which of course included Glastonbury, the "three miles east", have been found, but apparently there was an agreement indicating that some sort of payment had been made, for 65 years later, in 1671, certain Wethersfield and Glastonbury men paid several Indian Leaders 12 yards of "trading cloth" to sign, with their marks, a confirmatory deed to the original sale. This was recorded in the Wethersfield land records and reads, in part, as follows:

"..... and six milles in length by the Riuer side on the east side of the said Conecticot Riuer, from Pewter Pott brooke, north, to the Bounds betwene Weathersfield and Middletowne, south; the said Great Riuer west, the wholle leanth to runn three large milles into the wilderness east; the which lands, as afore said, hath been quietly possessed by the English now for seuerall yeeres past; but, in as much as there is noe written deed found under the hand of the said Sowheag, which may be an ocasion of trouble hereafter, for the preuention of which, knowing what our predeceassers haue don, and what hee had receiued for the same; and for the consideration of twelue yards of trading cloth, giuen to us a gratuity, by Capt. Samuel Wyllys, Mr. Henry Wollcot, Mr. James Richards, Capt. Samuell Welles, Mr. Samuel Tallcot[15], Mr. John Chester, Mr. James Treat, in the name and behalfe, and for the use of all others, the rest of the seuerall proprietors of the said land with in the limites of the Towneship of Weathersfield, aforesaid: We, Turramugus, Sepannamaw Squaw, daughter to Sowheage; Speunno, Nabowhee, Weesumshie, Waphanck; true heirs of and rightful sucksessers to the aforesaid Sowheage — hath fully confirmed, and doe by these presents fully and absolutely confirme the aforesaid grant made by our predeseasser, Sowheage, afore menssioned, enfeeoffed, sett ouer and confirmed ..... To haue and to hold all the aforesaid tract of lands, as they are bounded, with all the meaddowes, pastere, woods, under-woods, mines, mineralls, stones, qurrys, profits, comoditys, priulidges and appertinances, whatsoeuer, that are or may bee to the same belonging.

Samuel Welles's father was Thomas Welles, who was twice governor of Connecticut in the 17th century.[16] According to Henry Stiles, William Richard Cutter, and no doubt other genealogists, Thomas was born in 1598 in Essex, England. A number of genealogists, including James Savage, and Donald Lines Jacobus and Edgar Francis Waterman, give no birth date or place for Thomas. Donna Holt Siemiatkowski has a list of 12 common errors concerning Thomas, which include the claims that he was born about 1598, and in Essex. She says it has been established that he was born in or near Whichford, Warwickshire, around 1590, in a family which had been in Warwickshire for at least four generations, and which owned property but was not included among the gentry. Thus it appears that some of the males in his line were of that group known rather vaguely as yeomen.

The first wife of Thomas Welles, and the mother of all his children, was Alice Tomes. At one time some people thought Alice had a royal descent, but Donna Siemiatkowski discusses how this theory has been exploded. No confirmed royal line for Thomas has been found, either.

According to Jacobus and Waterman, Thomas Welles and his wife Alice arrived in New England in 1635 and settled in Hartford CT. According to Henry Stiles, they arrived probably about 1636, probably in Boston MA or vicinity, then perhaps went to Saybrook CT, and from there to Hartford (1637 or earlier), and then in 1643 to Wethersfield CT. Donna Siemiatkowski says it is incorrect, as reported for example by Rev. Alonzo Chapin in 1853, that Thomas was a private secretary to Lord Say and Sele, who was a prominent backer of colonization by the English along the Connecticut River, including what became the town of Saybrook. It seems Thomas may never have gone to Saybrook at all. She says Thomas arrived **"with his wife and six childen in the late summer 1636 and settled first in the Boston area, probably Cambridge"**, and that he **"probably came to Hartford with Thomas Hooker's party in June 1636."** This may leave you wondering when the late summer of 1636 occurred.

Thomas Welles possessed considerable clerical skills. In 1637, at a meeting of the governing body of Connecticut known as the General Court, he began a long career of public service when he was chosen as its clerk, and as one of its magistrates. This was the first session of the court independent of the authority of the Massachusetts Bay Colony. At this first meeting of the General Court, the towns of Windsor, Hartford and Wethersfield were given their present names. A few meetings later, the members of the court declared war on the Pequot Indians. I have already said enough about the Pequots.

Thomas remained a magistrate until he became Deputy-Governor of Connecticut in 1654 (some say until he died in 1660). Two years or so after he first became a magistrate, he became Treasurer of the Colony of Connecticut, an office he held in four different years. Two years later, in 1641, he became Secretary of the Colony, an office to which he was elected in five different years. He was elected Deputy-Governor of Connecticut in 1654, 1656, 1657 and 1659, and Governor of Connecticut in 1655 and 1658.

The genealogist R. R. Hinman wrote in 1846:

No one of the distinguished men of his time was more uniformly attentive to all his official duties than Gov. Welles, from his first appointment in 1637, until 1659. He was a constant attendant upon the General Court, except when employed in other public duties. His whole public life being fairly examined, he was as important a prop to the new colony as any of the principal men, except Gov. Winthrop — He died in 1660, and left a large estate to his children, viz. Thomas, Ichabod, Samuel, Jonathan, Joseph, Rebecca and Sarah." ..... Gov. Welles came to Massachusetts in a vessel named the Susan and Ellen, E. Payne, master, in company with Richard Saltonstall, Esq., and family, Walter Thornton and others." On the other hand, Donna Holt Siemiatkowski observed in 1990 in her genealogy of this Welles family that: "At least one other Thomas Welles came to Boston in 1635. This second man we now know as Thomas Welles of Ipswich. He is probably the Thomas who came on the "Susan and Ellen".

Thomas Welles was a magistrate and clerk of the General Court when the document known as the Fundamental Orders of Connecticut was promulgated in 1639. Other members of the committee which composed it were Roger Ludlow (a lawyer), John Haynes (the first, some say the second, governor of Connecticut), John Steel and Edward Hopkins (the second, some say the first, governor of Connecticut). It is often said that the Fundamental Orders contained the world's first written constitution, and that it for the first time anywhere placed the authority of government in the people. However, this appears to be a considerable overstatement.

In his discussion of the Fundamental Orders, the historian Charles M. Andrews, in the second volume of his four volume history of the American colonial period, published in 1936, observes first of all: "That Ludlow shaped the instrument in its final form can hardly be questioned. Its brevity, clarity, and compactness are the earmarks of an exceptionally good legal mind, wholly unlike the verboseness of the average Puritan writer." So much for average Puritan writers.

As to the matter of authority of the people, and concerning those who could vote, Andrews says:

This matter of the franchise at the beginnings of Connecticut's history has been greatly misunderstood. Apparently it has been assumed that every male adult in the colony was given a right to a share in government and that in the exercise of that right the majority rules. Nothing could be farther from the truth. The Fundamental Orders, as well as later laws, make a sharp distinction between one who voted in the town and one who voted for colony officers, that is, between an "admitted inhabitant" and a "freeman," though they are none too clear as to the precise qualifications of each. An "admitted inhabitant" was any householder of "honest conversation," whatever that may mean, who had taken a carefully phrased oath of fidelity to the commonwealth, which by the words used, "Soe helpe me God in our Lord Jesus Christe," testifies that it could be taken only by a Trinitarian. When admitted by majority vote of those properly qualified in town meeting, he could take part in local affairs, join in the election of local officials, and vote for deputies to the general court. But being an "admitted inhabitant" did not make a man a "freeman." The latter was any "admitted inhabitant" who had been selected for freemanship either by the general court itself or by some one or more of the magistrates who was authorized by the court to make "freemen." Only when thus admitted to freemanship could the adult male householder offer himself for election as a deputy, vote for the higher officials of the colony and himself fill the post of magistrate. Only a "freeman" could attend the court of election, either in person, or by proxy in case he lived in a distant town. Thus the "admitted inhabitants" were the householders in the towns, including also the adult males, married or unmarried, in their families, who as landowners and Trinitarians, were the substantial and godly men in their respective communities; the "freemen" were only such of the "admitted inhabitants" as were deemed by the general court fir to take part in the affairs of the commonwealth itself. As neither women, servants, apprentices, nor wnyone convicted of a scandalous offense were allowed to exercise the franchise or to have any part in the government of town or colony, it happened from the beginning that in the actual working out of the system the words "people: and :inhabitants" acquired a meaning much more restricted than that commonly given to them today. .....

Their notion of the "consent of the people: was not the consent of all the inhabitants but rather the consent of those only who, according to the Puritan idea, were of a "religious carriage," and therefore by God's will most qualified to give such consent. Numbers and majorities, though recognized as necessary to an ultimate decision, had very little to do with the running of the government. ..... To the Puritan what we call democracy was looked upon as an aberration of the human mind, disapproved of God and his faithful elect; and only those who were Christians, of honest and peaceable conversation, substantial, respectable, and reliable fathers in Israel were considered worthy to build up a community the design of which was religious." Neither Baptists nor Quakers were eligible to be freemen, and early on were usually not even admissible inhabitants.

As to the Fundamental Orders being the first written constitution in the world, or even in New England, Andrews observes:

The Fundamental Orders, as far as defining the functions of a government is concerned, are very imperfect and incomplete and scarcely go beyong a statement of what the framework of such a system should be. They are much less elaborate than is the outline drawn up by John Cotton in 1636, representing the government of Massachusetts, or than the New Haven "fundamentals" of 1639 and 1643. [The New Haven colony was at that time separate from Connecticut.]

In a collection of articles by various people, intended for use in schools, published in 1934, two years before his four volume history of New England, Andrews says:

The Fundamental Orders are a constitution or civil compact in the same sense that any body of law that defines a government has a constitutional character. It is not a constitution analogous to our federal Constitution or to our state constitution of today, nor was it ever taken as a model for any of the constitutions of modern times. Nevertheless, it is a document of which Connecticut is deservedly proud, for it represents the first formal attempt, in the history of this country or any country, to draft a frame of popular self-government, free from any power over and outside of the colony itself.

It seems that Andrews made a closer study of the significance of the Fundamental Orders after he wrote this. Or, more likely, historians write differently in textbooks for schools than they do in their work intended for grown-ups.

It appears, then, that some of the descendants of Thomas Welles, and other people, may have exaggerated the place of the Fundamental Orders in political history. It *does* seem to be true, however, that in 1641, when Thomas Welles was Secretary of the General Court, he made a copy of the Fundamental Orders in his own handwriting.

The Charter of the Colony of Connecticut, promulgated in 1662, made the Fundamental Orders obsolete. Thomas Welles is mentioned several times in this document, in company with numerous other prominent people of the colony, including several other ancestors of mine. However, Thomas did not live to enjoy seeing his name in the Charter. He died in 1660. "**Gov. Winthrop,**" says Henry Stiles, "**in a letter dated 3 Apl., 1660, mentions Gov. W.'s dth. as having been very sudden, "being very well at supper, and dead before midnight."** "

The genealogists Donald Lines Jacobus and Edgar Francis Waterman took the actions of some relatives of Thomas Welles as occasion to argue for the importance of genealogy in historical studies:

John Tomes, son of John and Alice . . . married first, Ellen (Gunne) Phelps, widow of Joseph Phelps of Bengeworth, co. Worcester, and daughter of Richard and Anne (Fulwood) Gunne; married second, at Wormington, co. Gloucester, 3 Aug. 1601, Ann Warner. . . . By the first wife, he had four daughters, Mary, Anne, Joan, and Alice. By the second wife, he had a son, John, born about Oct. 1602. It was the latter who concealed Charles II in his home when the king was a fugitive after the battle of Worcester, on the night of 10 Sept. 1651. He was disguised as servant of Mrs. Jane Lane, and as "Will Jackson" was sent to the kitchen. The maid, getting supper for her master's friends, asked him to wind up the Jack. Will Jackson obediently attempted it, but hit not the right way, and the annoyed maid asked, "What county

man are you, that you know not how to wind up a Jack?" He answered to her satisfaction, "I am a poor tenant's son of Colonel Lane in Staffordshire. We seldom have roast meat, but when we have we don't make use of a Jack." . . . . .

The importance of genealogy to historical study has sometimes been sneered at, but so far as we are aware, the part which the Welles genealogy played in the obtaining of Connecticut's Charter has never been told. After the restoration of Charles II to the throne in 1660, both Connecticut and New Haven, neither colony then having any legal status except such as the suffrage of their own freemen gave them, hastened to apply for a royal charter. New Haven was suspected, and justly, by the new monarch, of having harbored the "regicides," and not only failed to obtain a charter, but found its territory included in the Connecticut Charter of 1662.

The statesmanship of Gov. John Winthrop has been deservedly praised for his success in obtaining this liberal charter from the king. It is to be taken for granted that Winthrop played every card which he held in his hand. Thomas and Alice (Tomes) Welles were then dead, but their family still lived in the colony, and one of Winthrop's aces must have been the fact that Mrs. Welles's brother, John Tomes, had given refuge to the king when he was a fugitive. This is not mere theory; it can be demonstrated by a study of the names of the nineteen men who were specified in the charter itself as patentees.

Of these, Thomas Welles was the eldest surviving son of Gov. Thomas and Alice (Tomes) Welles; Anthony Howkins was their son-in-law; and John Deming was brother of Gov. Welles's second wife [Elizabeth Deming]. The wife of Samuel Welles, youngest son of Alice Tomes, whom he married only in 1659, was granddaughter of Richard Treat, another patentee, who was father-in-law both of John Deming [brother of Elizabeth Deming], already mentioned, and of Matthew Campfield, still another patentee. Thus five out of the nineteen, more than a fourth of the patentees, were closely connected with the Welles family. That this heavy representation was not a matter of chance is deduced from the fact that the younger Thomas Welles before he was named in the charter had never held any civil post in the colonial government, while Howkins, although elected a Deputy for falf a dozen terms, had not at that time been promoted to the "Upper House" as a Governor's Assistant. With them, at any rate, we may conclude that the Tomes connection, and the use Winthrop made of the king's gratitude, were the reasons why they were named as patentees. We may conclude further that the Tomes connection with Connecticut Colony was one of the aces which Winthrop providentially found in his hand when he negotiated the Royal Charter. The people of New Haven Colony might treasonably shelter the regicides, but Winthrop could point out that the uncle of Mr. Welles and Mrs. Howkins had proved his loyalty when the king was in desperate straits, and that the people of Connecticut were generally of that stripe. And Connecticut received a charter which included the territory of New Haven as well! Decidedly, "genealogy is the handmaid of history,"- -when it is the Welles genealogy.

In the *Journal* of John Winthrop (1587-1649), sometimes known as *The History of New England from 1630 to 1649,* the name of Thomas Welles (or Wells) doesn't appear. Nor is a biography of Thomas Welles to be found in

Book II of Volume I of the *Magnalia Christi Americana* of Cotton Mather (1702), which is entitled "**Containing the Lives of the Governors and Names of the Magistrates of New-England.**" Gov. Thomas Welles is mentioned only once in the *Magnalia*, when Mather remarks on the successors of the early governors John Haynes and Edward Hopkins. "**And besides these .....,**" says Mather, "**there were Mr. Willis, Mr. Wells, and Mr. Webster, all of whom also had opportunity to express their liberal and generous dispositions, and the *governing virtues* of wisdom, justice and courage, by the election of the freemen in the colony before its being united with New Haven.**"

In his history of Connecticut published in 1818, Benjamin Trumbull notes that after 1659, Thomas Welles appears no more as a magistrate and officer of the Connecticut colony. This is of course because he died in 1660, before the election of that year. Trumbull has a footnote:

Four or five governors of Connecticut, governor Haynes, governor Wyllys, governors Wells and Webster, lie buried at Hartford, without a monument. William Leet, Esq. governor of New Haven and Connecticut, also lies interred there, in the same obscure manner. Considering their many and important public services, this is remarkable; but their virtues have embalmed their names, and will render them venerable to the latest posterity.

In 1837, the Ancient Burying Ground Association of Hartford erected a monument which contains names of the Founders of Hartford, which somehow come out to be an even 100. Thomas Welles is among them.

Donna Holt Siemiatkowsi says:

He became involved in the establishment of the settlement at Stratford, named to the town near his home village in England. His son John was sent to oversee his interests there. According to tradition, the last child of Thomas and Alice, a son named Joseph, was born shortly after their arrival in Connecticut. Primary documentary evidence for this son has not yet surfaced. He apparently did not survive as he is not mentioned in his father's will. However, he lived long enough to have his memory perpetuated in the name of some of his sibling's descendants. A few years later Alice died, not having reached the age of fifty. In 1646 Thomas married Elizabeth Foote, widow of Nathaniel Foote who died in Wethersfield in 1643, and sister of Joseph Deming of Wethersfield. She was unwilling to leave the homestead of many acres she was managing after her husband's death. As a result, one of the highest officers in the colony left his home in the center of Hartford and moved to Wethersfield with his younger children, Samuel and Sarah who were raised [with] her younger children Frances, Sarah, and Rebecca.

Thomas wrote his will on 7 Nov 1659. He seemed to be in good health on the evening of 14 Jan 1659/60, being well after supper, but dead by midnight. His will left his wife the use of half his housing and orchard, with her own land to return to her. His own land and house went to his grandson Robert, the only child of his

oldest son to live in Wethersfield. He left land to sons Samuel and Thomas, and to Thomas son of the deceased son John, 20 pounds to Thomas, Samuel, Mary's children, Anne, Sarah, and 10 pounds to Mary Robbins' children. Elizabeth lived another 22 years, leaving her estate to her children and grandchildren by Nathaniel Foote. [17]

13. Jonathan Hale I, II and III.

Jonathan Hale, son of Samuel Hale and Mary Welles dealt with above, was born in Glastonbury Ct in 1696 and died there in 1772. He married Sarah Talcott in 1717. She died in 1743, and Jonathan married second Hannah (Chester) Welles who died in 1749, and third Mary (White) Hollister who died in 1780, after Jonathan's death. Hannah Welles was the widow of Gideon Welles, and Mary Hollister was the widow of Joseph Hollister.[18]

Donald Lines Jacobus and Edgar Francis Waterman say in their *Hale, House and Related Families, Mainly of the Connecticut River Valley*:

Jonathan Hale was appointed Ensign of the Glastonbury Train Band, May 1730. He was commissioned Lieutenant of the first Company in Glastonbury, May 1738, and Captain of the same, May 1743. He served as Deputy for Glastonbury to the Connecticut General Assembly, May and Oct. 1736, May and Oct. 1737, May and Oct. 1738, May and Oct. 1739, May, July, Oct. and Nov. 1740, May and Oct, 1741, May and Oct. 1742, May and Oct. 1743, May and Oct. 1744, Feb., Mar. May, July, Aug. and Oct. 1745, May and Oct. 1746, Jan. and Oct. 1747, May and Oct. 1748, May and Oct. 1749, May, Oct. and Nov. 1750, Oct. 1751, May and Oct. 1752, Oct. 1753, May 1754, May, Aug. and Oct. 1755, Jan., Feb. and Mar. 1756, May 1762, Oct. 1763, and Mar. 1764; and acted on several important legislative committees. He also served as colonial Auditor, in 1737, 1739, 1740, 1741, 1742, and 1745, He was a Justice of the Peace from 1739 until his death in 1772, over thirty-three years, one of the longest periods of continuous service in that office in colonial Connecticut. ... ... The will of Jonathan Hale of Glastonbury, dated 30 Nov. 1771, proved 15 July 1772, named his eldest son Jonathan Hale (my negro man Newport, etc.); sons Elizur, David and Theodore Hale; only daughter Prudence Blake; wife Mary Hale (movable estate she brought with her when I married her); daughters-in-law [step-daughters] Eunice Parsons and the widow Sarah Woodbridge (my negro woman that was their mother's).

Jonathan Hale was the most prominent member of his family in his generation, and was active in land dealings... ... In 1729, 1730, 1731, 1749 and 1750, he was on a committee to survey and lay out town lands.

His epitaph:

Here lies Interred the Remains of Jonathan Hale, Esq., who having served his Generation in Several Offices of Trust with Faithfulness, fell asleep, July 16, A. D. 1772, in the 76th year of his Age.

Jonathan Hale, the son of the foregoing Jonathan Hale, was born in 1720/1721 in Glastonbury CT and died on 7 Mar 1776 in Jamaica Plains MA. The Rev. Alonzo B. Chapin, D.D. reports in his *Glastenbury for Two Hundred Years, A Centennial Discourse, May 18th A.D. 1853*:

"CITIZENS OF GLASTENBURY WHO DIED IN THE REVOLUTIONARY WAR ... ...

From Glastenbury Church Records .....

1776, Mar. 7, Capt. Jonathan Hale, died in the army at Jamaica Plains, Roxbury, Massachusetts Bay.

......

1776, Oct. 1, Jonathan Hale, died a few days after he returned sick from the army."

The Jonathan Hale who died 1 Oct 1776 was the son of the Jonathan Hale who died 7 Mar 1776, i.e. the grandson of the Jonathan Hale who died 16 Jul 1772. The eldest Jonathan, Jonathan Hale I, managed to die, evidently peacefully, some 4 years before his son, Jonathan Hale II, and grandson Jonathan Hale III, died in the Revolutionary War, the United States War of Independence, Jonathan II at age 56 and Jonathan III at age 31.

From the *PICTORIAL FIELD BOOK OF THE REVOLUTION*, volume I, by Benson J. Lossing, 1850:

The design of Washington to fortify Dorchester Heights was kept a profound secret, and, to divert the attention of Howe, the Americans opened a severe bombardment and cannonade on the night of the 2d of March [1776] from the several batteries at Lechmere's Point, Roxbury, Cobble and Plowed Hills, and Lamb's Dam. Several houses in the city were shattered, and six British soldiers killed. The fire was returned with spirit, but with out serious effect. In the course of the bombardment, the Americans burst the "Congress" thirteen inch mortar, another of the same size, and three ten inch mortars.

On Sunday and Monday nights [March 3, 4, 1776] a similar cannonade was opened upon the city. At seven o'clock on Monday evening, General Thomas, with two thousand men, and intrenching tools, proceeded to take possession of Dorchester Heights. A train of three hundred carts, laden with fascines and hay, followed the troops. Within an hour, marching in perfect silence, the detachment reached the heights. It was separated into two divisions, and upon the two eminences already mentioned they commenced throwing up breast-works. Bundles of hay were placed on the town side of Dorchester Neck to break the rumble of the carts passing to and fro, and as a defense against the guns of the enemy, if they should be brought to bear upon the troops passing the Neck. Notwithstanding the moon was shining brightly and the air was serene, the laborers were not observed by the British sentinels Under the direction of the veteran Gridley, the engineer at Bunker Hill, they worked wisely and well. Never was more work done in so short a time, and at dawn two forts were raised sufficiently high to afford ample protection for the forces within. They presented a formidable aspect to the

alarmed Britons. Howe, overwhelmed with astonishment, exclaimed, "I know not what I shall do. The rebels have done more in one night than my whole army would have done in a month." They had done more than merely raise embankments; cannons were placed upon them, and they now completely commanded the town, placing Britons and Tories in the utmost peril.

The morning on which these fortresses were revealed to the enemy was the memorable 5th of March, the anniversary of the *Boston Massacre*. The associations connected with the day nerved the Americans to more vigorous action, and they determined to celebrate and signalize the time by an act of retributive vengeance. Howe saw and felt his danger; and his anxiety was augmented when Admiral Shuldham assured him that the British fleet in the harbor must be inevitably destroyed when the Americans should get their heavy guns and mortars upon the heights. Nor was the army in the city secure. It was therefore resolved to take immediate measures to dislodge the provincials. Accordingly, two thousand four hundred men were ordered to embark in transports, rendezvous at Castle William, and, under the gallant Earl Percy, make an attack that night upon the rebel works. Washington was made acquainted with this movement, and, supposing the attack was to be made immediately, sent a re-enforcement of two thousand men to General Thomas. Labor constantly plied its hands in strengthening the works. As the hills on which the redoubts were reared were very steep, rows of barrels, filled with loose earth, were placed outside the breast-works, to be rolled down upon the attacking column so as to break their ranks; a measure said to have been suggested by Mifflin. All was now in readiness. It was a mild, sunny day. The neighboring heights were crowded with people, expecting to see the bloody tragedy of Breed's Hill acted again. Washington himself repaired to the intrenchments, and encouraged the men by reminding them that it was the 5th of March. The commander-in-chief and the troops were in high spirits, for they believed the long-coveted conflict and victory to be near.

While these preparations were in progress on Dorchester Heights, four thousand troops, in two divisions, under Generals Sullivan and Greene, were parading at Cambridge, ready to be led by Putnam to an attack on Boston when Thomas's batteries should give the signal. They were to embark in boats in the Charles River, now clear of ice, under cover of three floating batteries, and, assaulting the city at two prominent points, to force their way to the works on the Neck, open the gates, and let in the troops from Roxbury.

Both parties were ready for action in the afternoon; but a furious wind that had arisen billowed the harbor, and rolled such a heavy surf upon the shore where the boats of the enemy were obliged to land, that it was unsafe to venture. During the night the rain came down in torrents, and a terrible storm raged all the next day. Howe abandoned his plan, and Washington, greatly disappointed, returned to his camp, leaving a strong force to guard the works on Dorchester Heights.

The situation of Howe was now exceedingly critical. The fleet and army were in peril, and the loyal inhabitants, greatly terrified, demanded that sure protection which Howe had so often confidently promised. He called a council of officers on the 7th [March, 1776], when it was resolved to save the army by evacuating the town. This resolution spread great consternation among the Tories in the city, for they dreaded the just indignation of the patriots when they should return. They saw the power on which they had leaned as almost invincible growing weak, and quailing before those whom it had affected to despise. They well knew that severe retribution for miseries which they had been instrumental in inflicting, surely awaited them, when British bayonets should leave the peninsula and the excited patriots should return to their desolated homes. The dangers of a perilous voyage to a strange land seemed far less fearful than the indignation of the oppressed Americans, and the Loyalists resolved to brave the former rather than the latter. They began, therefore, to prepare for a speedy departure; merchandise, household furniture, and private property of every kind were crowded on board the ships. Howe had been advised by Dartmouth, in November, to evacuate Boston, but excused himself by pleading that the shipping was inadequate. He was now obliged to leave with less, and, in addition to his troops, take with him more than one thousand refugee Loyalists, and their effects. Ammunition and war-like magazines of all kinds were hurried on board the vessels; heavy artillery, that could not be carried away, was dismounted, spiked, or thrown into the sea, and some of the fortifications were demolished. The number of ships and transports was about one hundred and fifty; but these were insufficient for the conveyance of the multitude of troops and inhabitants, their most valuable property, and the quantity of military stores to be carried away.

[1] William Pynchon is one of my 9th great-grandfathers. The Reverend Henry Smith is one of my 8th great-grandfathers. The other Henry Smith and John Winthrop appear to be unrelated to me.

[2] This indecision of Samuel's as to 1636 and 1637 seems not to have been the result of concern about the old style of dating, in which new years were taken to begin on 25 March rather than 1 January, since the change in styles didn't take place in England and its colonies until 1752. When one writes, say, 1662/1663, this may be taken to mean 1662 old style, 1663 new style. This contrasts with 1662-1663, which customarily means 1662 through 1663, or from some time in 1662 to some time in 1663, referring only to new style dating.

[3] Another witch, Rebecca Greensmith, is a 10th great-grandmother of mine. Rebecca first married Abraham Elson (or Elson) who is my corresponding 10th great-grandfather. She then married Jarvis Mudge who is conceivably an ancestor of another Jarvis Mudge who married a Prudence Treat who is a 3rd cousin 7 times removed of mine. She then married Nathaniel Greensmith, and she and Nathaniel were executed for witchcraft by hanging, in Hartford CT in 1662/1663. The historian William DeLoss Love says:

The indictment read:

Nathaniel Greensmith, thou art here indicted by the name of Nathaniel Greensmith for not having the feare of God before thine eyes; thou hast entertained familiarity with Satan, the grand Enemy of God and Mankind, and by his help hast acted things in a preter naturall way beyond human abilities in a naturall course, for which according to ye Law of God and ye established laws of this Commonwealth thou deserveth to die.

The form of the information, used in the Superior Court for many years, assigned all crimes to the instigation of the Devil. The magistrates at this trial were as follows: Mr. [Matthew] Allyn [an 11th ggf = great-grandfather of mine], moderator, Mr [Samuel] Wyllys, Mr [Richard] Treat [9th ggf if Richard Treat 1584-1669, but may be son Richard Treat 1662/3-c1662, brother of Joanna TREAT, 8th ggm], Mr.[Henry] Woolcot [i.e. Wolcott, 8th and also 9th ggf], Danll Clark, Sec., Mr. Jo. Allyn [son of Matthew ALLYN]. The jury were: Edw. Griswold [son of 8th ggf George Griswold], Walter Ffiler Ensign [Nicholas] Olmstead [sic: this may mean Walter Ffiler, Ensign and Nicholas Olmstead --- I have a 9th ggf James ENSIGN who married Sarah Elson, daughter of the witch Rebecca (Elson) (Mudge) Greenleaf; Nicholas OLMSTEAD was father-in-law of Hannah MIX, sister of 7th ggf Daniel (1) MIX)], Samll Boreman, Goodm [Gregory] Winterton, John Cowles [8th ggf], Samll Marshall, Samll Hale [8th ggf – this is the Samuel Hale, Sr., dealt with above], Nathan Willet, John Hart, John Wadsworth, Robert Webster. The execution of the criminals then devolved upon the Marshal, who was Jonathan Gilbert. One of the accused is said to have seen this worthy official in a dream, which seemed to presage the end. He was the first of three appointed to settle Greensmith's estate. Jonathan Gilbert succeeded Thomas Stanton in this office, and was followed by George Grave.

See http://inmatesofwillard.com/2012/07/19/my-8th-great-grandmother-the-witch-of-hartford-connecticut/ (accessed Jul 2013)

[4] Adams notes: "The General Court of the Colony in the Code of 1650, declares that "the most Aunciernt Towne for the [Connecticut] River is determined by the Court to bee Wethersfield," and this declaration was reiterated in the Revision of 1672. They said it twice, so I suppose it must be so. Rev. Stephen was a son of my 8th great-grandfather Thomas Mix (or Meekes))

[5] Adams notes: "The General Court of the Colony in the Code of 1650, declares that "the most Aunciernt Towne for the [Connecticut] River is determined by the Court to bee Wethersfield," and this declaration was reiterated in the Revision of 1672. They said it twice, so I suppose it must be so. Rev. Stephen was a son of my 8th great-grandfather Thomas Mix (or Meekes)).

[6] A 7th cousin 2 times removed of mine.

[7] The one who is one of my 7th great-grandfathers.

[8] Esther Cowles, a daughter of one of my 8th great-grandfathers, John Cowles, married the son Thomas Bull (Jr) of Thomas Bull. Hannah Mix, a daughter of one of my 8th great-grandfathers Thomas Mix, married the son Thomas of Nicholas Olmstead (as Omsted was more commonly spelled).

[9] The Reverend Samuel Stone mentioned here is one of my 7th great-grandfathers.

[10] No relation, as far as I know, to the Reverend Samuel Stone.

[11] Another book about the Pequots has appeared, *The Revenge of the Pequots* by Kim Isaac Eisler, 2001. Eisler reports:
"**On October 18, 1994, in the small town of Ledyard, Connecticut, the chief of the richest and most powerful Native American tribe in the United States strode purposefully into the white construction trailer that served as his temporary office and waited while an operator connected him to the White House. ... ... At 10:18 A.M., the familiar sound of Bill Clinton's voice came over the line. ... ... Clinton began by thanking [tribal chief Richard "Skip"] Hayward for his past generosity, for the chief had recently contributed nearly $500,000 dollars to the Democratic Party to support candidates in the 1994 congressional elections. Hayward told the president how much he had supported his and his wife Hillary's health-care initiatives, and volunteered a little bit of information about the federally designed tribal health-insurance plan. He expressed his hope that the president would support the tribe's request to the Department of the Interior and the Bureau of Indian Affairs for help in building a health clinic for members of the fast-growing Pequot tribe. "We're going to do everything we can to help you," Clinton promised, emphasizing the word "you" in his distinctive Arkansas accent. Hayward also expressed his concern that the president be sensitive about issues of Indian sovereignty and not support any efforts to tax the giant gambling casino that his tribe had recently begun operating. The conversation ended amiably with**

Clinton's assurances on that score ... ... Hayward leaned back in exultation. ... ...
In the hundred years since their brutal forced relocation to reservations,
American Indians had come to live in abject poverty ... ... in 1994, for the first time
in the history of Native American relations, it was not a tribe that was seeking
federal help, but the president of the United States asking to be the beneficiary of
Indian wealth.

[12] One of Lt. Samuel's children by his second wife, Mary, was Jonathan Hale. Lt. Samuel and Mary are 6th great-grandparents of mine, and Jonathan and his wife Elizabeth Welles are 5th great-grandparents of mine.

[13] One of my 9th great-grandfathers.

[14] Thomas Mix was one of my 8th great-grandfathers. A write-up on Thomas Mix by Newell A. Williams was sent to Ed Chesney by Williams in 1983, and relayed to me later on the Internet:

Thomas Mix

The normal picture, that we have, of the Puritans that settled New England is that of sober, law-abiding, industrious men and women. In fact often they seem too good to be true. This little story will, to some extent, change that, and perhaps make them seem more human. The founder of the Mix family in America was Thomas Mix. The name was spelled Meekes in the early New Haven records. Later he signed a report as Thom. Mexx. From whence he came, we do not know. He was first mentioned in the New Haven records in 1647.

To set the stage for our story, let's talk a bit about Nathaniel Turner. He also is an ancestor of ours. He more nearly fits the picture of the brave, hardy Puritan pioneer. Captain Turner was one of the original founders of New Haven in 1639. He was a man of some means. His net worth was estimated to be 800 pounds in 1643. One of the more well-to-do planters, he helped explore the land in Connecticut as far west as the Hudson River, where he made contact with the Dutch of New Amsterdam. There is some indication that he went as far as the Delaware River into what is now Pennsylvania.

New Haven was a seaport, and some of the richer men decided to build a ship to promote trade with the other colonies and England. It was finished, and in January of 1646 it sailed for England with Captain Turner on board. It was never heard of again. Two hundred years later, Longfellow wrote a poem commemorating the tragic voyage. Turner left his wife an estate of about 450 pounds including a debt of 14 pounds owed her by Thomas Mix. He also left her with several children, one of whom was a daughter named

Rebecca. Later Mrs. Turner remarried [this time] a Mr. Samuel Goodanhousen, a Dutchman, presumably from New Amsterdam.

In 1649 Thomas and Rebecca got into trouble, or to put it more bluntly, Thomas got Rebecca in trouble. The following is a direct quote from the New Haven Colonial Record:

"Thomas Meekes and Rebecka Turner was called before ye court to answer to their sinfull miscariag [sic] in matter of fornication, with sundry lyes added therto by them both in grose and hainiouse manner. The matter hauing bine formerly heard before the gouerner in a private way, wch was now declared to ye court in ther prsenc, and they called to answer. Thomas Meekes said he could say nothing against whath bine declared but it is true, and he desires to judge and condeme himself for it in ye sight of God and his people. And for Rebecka Turner, she acknowledg the things ye charged was true, and though she had saide Thomas Meekes had had to do with her but once, yett it was oftener, as she now saith."

There was further testimony which implied that Rebecka had had an affair with another man [a Mr. Westerhousen], as the governor told the court:

"The Gouerner told ye court that they haue heard ye severall passages of ye busines concerning Thomas Meekes and Rebecka Turner, wherin beside ye fornication ther hath bine much impudenc in lying, espicially one his pte [on his part], calling God to witness ye truth of a thing wch himselfe knew to be false, as he now professeth. Allso ye passages concerning Mr. Westerhousen, and what is proved vpon oath, yett not owned by him, which leaves the court much vnsatisfyed.

"Matters being thus prepared, before ye court proceeded sentence, Mr. Goodanhousen desired to speake, and desired the court to consider that Rebecka is weake and haath sore breasts with a froward child, that therfore, if it may be, thay would spare corporall punishment, and if they laid a fine he would see it paid.

"The court having heard and weighed what was spoken, proceeded, and ordered that Thomas Meekes be severely whipped for his folly of sinful vncleanness, and for lying and misscariages that way be fined 5 pounds.

"For Rebecka Turner that she also be whipped, if in referenced [sic] to her self and child it may stand wth due mercy, but upon a view and search by midwife sister Kimberly, the court saw cause to forbeare that, and ordered her to paye a fine of 10 pounds, wch Mr. Goodanhousen Promised [sic] to paye for her."

It can be stated here that Thomas and Rebecka were married. Under the circumstances, they had no other choice, but this did not end their troubles.

A year or so after the above trial, a Richard Fido and Nicholas Sloper, indentured servants of neighbors of Thomas Meekes, were charged with theft, lying, disorderly night meetings, drinking "strong watter" and having feasts at night on stollen food from their master. The testimony brought Clements, who persuaded them to steal a pistol from one of their masters. Clements later sold it to an Indian for 12 shillings.

Clements was a friend of Thomas Meekes, and introduced the two servants to him. Clements suggested to Sloper that he live with Thomas, after his term of servitude expired, stating "It was the best place he had found." At times the servants would steal meat from their masters, and bring it to the Meekes' house. Here Rebecka would cook it, and they would eat and drink until late at night.

About this time the two servants stole a heifer. They cut off its ears, so that the identifying marks could not be seen. Then they sold it to Thomas. Several days later the heifer escaped and returned to its rightful owner. Thomas knew where it was, but made no attempt to claim it.

On being called to the court, and being charged with these inditements, Thomas answered as follows:

"It was true that James Clements did bring Fido and Sloper to sundrie meetings at his house, to drink strong watter, and eat some meate, also at one time he did receive a bushell of corne, and a peece or two of beefe wch Sloper brought wch they dressed for them to supper, and told Sloper that if his Mistress gave him leave he might come. As for the heiffer, when James went away he told him he had a heiffer he would sell him wch Richard's master gave him. So he bought the heiffer for 5 pounds and pd James 3 pounds and was to pay 40 shillings to Richard Fido. He kept her a while in his yard, but she gott out and went to Mr. Gibbard, and he going thither saw her in ye yard, but because he bought her nof of Fido, as well as James, he would not speak to Mr. Gibbard, till hee had spake with Fido, and when he spake with him, he vunderstood that they had stole the heiffer from Mr. Gibbard, yet upon his desire he promised to keepe it secrett. Thomas was told that servants could not own cattle, and that the ears had been clipped, should have told him that the heifer had been stolen. At this he was silent and could not answer, but said he desired to "owne his sinn."

"Rebecka Meekes, wife of Thomas Meekes, was called befor ye court and told that amone severall others, she was charged with partaking wth them in ther sinn, intertaining mens servants in ye nite season when their Gouerners were in bed, that she had satt and drunke strong watter wth them vnfitt for her sex in such season & in such manner, and when her husband had wth drawne, she hath kept them company, and received other stollen goods, and that it was a great agravation both in her and her husband, that it was so quickly after they were sentence in this court for other sinnful miscariags. She was bid to speak is she had anything to say to cleere herself. She answered she knew not what to say."

The court sentenced the two servants to be jailed, whipped, and to work off their debts & fines, as for Thomas & Rebecka:

"They are guilty of intertaining & inviting mens servants such as they might well suspect came in disorderly sinnful base way, in ye night when ther Gouernors were in bed, to drink strong watter, they also have received stollen goods, and that against ther light, for when Sloper brought the bushell of corne, he said it was not safe for him to receive it, yet did so. They buy a heiffer of 5 pound price wch they might vpon grounds declared to them, conceit [sic] she stollen, and when it was told them it was stole, yet then promised to conceal it. The Court considered what a micheivous example this is, and how dangerous it is to nourish vnrighteousness & disorder in a plantation.

"Therfore the sentenc of ye court is that Thomas Meekes paye twenty pownds a fine for these misdemenours and miscariages, and when Fido & Sloper is wipped, he and his wife are to come to ye whipping post, and stand ther, putting each of them one hand into ye hole of the post, and stand ther while ye others whipped: that they may haue part of ye shame wch ther sinn deserveth: and to give security for the fine, or paye it presently, and to paye the due charges of the prison..

"Mr. Goodanhouse before the court ingageth himselfe, for ye payment of this fine wthin a moneth: and ingageth himselfe in 10 pounds more, for the appearance of Thomas Meekes and his wife to fullfil the sentence of ye Court when Fido and Sloper are whipped."

Samuel Goodanhouse proved to be a good stepfather & stepfather-in-law to the two young people. They continued to live in New Haven, and with age became more respectable. Thomas later became a freeman and constable. He lived in New Haven 40 more years, and Rebecca lived until 1731, when she must have been around 100 years old.

Their son, Daniel, married Ruth Rockwell, daughter of John Rockwell, and great-granddaughter of Bernard Capen. My wife [i.e. Newell A. Williams' wife], Pauline Reed Williams, was of Capen ancestry, both on her mother's and father's side of the family. Our children can trace their lineage back to Bernard Capen through three families.

Daniel Mix was one of the first settlers of Wallingford, Connecticut. The Mix family lived there for over one hundred years. During this time they seemed to be closely associated with the Royce family, as there were several marriages between the two families. In the City of Wallingford, there is still the Royce House, which is preserved as a historical monument.

Josiah Mix married Keziah Royce (now changed to Rice). Josiah, who had been a Revolutionary War soldier, joined the great western migration, and moved to Rootstown, Portage County, Ohio, in 1816. Their graves can still be seen in the Old Rootstown Cemetery (1980).

Josiah's son, Samuel Rice Mix, grew up in Ohio, and was the father of Newell Mix. Newell Mix married Ruth Elizabeth Kent, and about 1875 moved to Varthage, Missouri. Ruth was birn in Southwick, Massachusetts, but grew up in Atwater, Ohio. She was on a visit to Southwick when she married Newell, who had been going to college in Massachusetts.

I never knew my grandfather, Newell Mix, but my grandmother Mix was everything a grandmother should be, a little old lady who lived in an old brick house with an old barn to play in. The house had a dark mysterious cellar, and a fascinating attic with all kinds of treasures. Above all, grandmother made the best cookies in the world for her ten year old grandson.
Newell A. Williams — August 22, 1981

Daniel Mix and Ruth Rockwell are 7th great-grandparents of mine (Gordon Fisher). They had a son Thomas Mix who married Deborah Royce. They aren't mentioned in Williams' letter. They are 6th great-grandparents of mine. They had a son Josiah Mix . This is not the same Josiah Mix listed by Williams. My Josiah Mix married Sybil Holt, and they are 5th great-grandparents of mine. The line to me then goes from these two to Jesse Mix who married Deborah Parker (4th ggp), and had a son also named Jesse Mix who married Polly (Mary) Burk (3rd ggp). Next was Luther Mix who married Lucia Elizabeth Billings (2nd ggp), and had a daughter Isadora Alfretta Mix who married Elvin Gilman Hill. These were my great-grandparents on my mother's side. Elvin Hill died in 1905. He was a corporal in the 1st Minnesota Volunteers during the Civil War of the temporarily dis-United States, and later owned and ran a sawmill in Little Elk MN, near Little Falls in central Minnesota. Isadora (Mix) Hill died in 1937 when I was 12 years old. She and my mother and I used to play three-handed bridge for a couple of years before she died, starting when I was 10 years old. My maternal grandmother was Adele Erdine Hill who married Ethan Sanford Brown, and their daughter, my mother, was Ione Adele Brown who married Tully McCrea Fisher.

[15] Samuel Talcott was one of my 7th great-grandfathers.

[16] Thomas Welles was one of my 8th great-grandfathers.

[17] Thomas Welles' first wife, Alice Tomes, died sometime before 1646, before she was 50 years old. In 1646, Thomas married Elizabeth Foote, née Deming, widow of Nathaniel Foote of Nathaniel Foote of Wethersfield CT. This eventually led to a curious genealogical result. Thomas Welles and Alice Tomes were 8th great-grandparents of mine by descents (more than one) through my father. His second wife was a 9th great-grandmother of mine, by way of her first husband, Nathaniel Foote, by descent through my mother. Thus it appears that my mother and father wcre 8th cousins, once removed, a fact that I'm sure was never known to them.

[18] Jonathan Hale and Sarah Talcott were 5th great-grandparents of mine. The first husband Gideon Welles of Jonathan's second wife, Hannah (Chester) Welles, was a son of Robert Welles and Elizabeth Goodrich who were 7th great-grandparents of mine. This Gideon

Welles was a 2nd cousin 3 times removed of the Gideon Welles who was Secretary of the Navy under Abraham Lincoln, and is a 6th great-granduncle of mine. (The other Gideon Welles is a 3rd cousin 4 times removed on mine.   The first husband Joseph Hollister of Jonathan's third wife is a grandson of John Hollister and Sarah Goodrich who are 7th great-grandparents of mine, and therefore a 1st cousin (though 7 times removed) of mine.

CPSIA information can be obtained at www.ICGtesting.com
Printed in the USA
LVOW09s0845041213

363723LV00025BB/1121/P

9 781484 106747